Place, Nature and Spirit:
A Lake District Experience

To Nickie,

With thanks,

Nigel
xx

(SUN. 16TH DEC. '12.)

Place, Nature and Spirit: A Lake District Experience

Nigel Hammett

Copyright ©2012, Nigel Hammett

All rights reserved. No part of this book may be reproduced, stored, or transmitted by any means—whether auditory, graphic, mechanical, or electronic—without written permission of both publisher and author, except in the case of brief excerpts used in critical articles and reviews. Unauthorized reproduction of any part of this work is illegal and is punishable by law.

ISBN 978-1-105-60866-7

Acknowledgements

The version of Wordsworth's poetry used in this book is the one published by Ward, Lock & Co. Ltd. The text follows that which he finally revised for the last collected edition issued in his lifetime.

In addition to the authors acknowledged in the text and detailed in the references, there are several other people who deserve thanks for their help in the production of this book. In the early stages of writing I received encouragement and professional advice from my friend, James Bilton. I have visited the Wordsworth Centre at Grasmere many times and made use of their exhibitions and library facilities. Special thanks are due to Jeff Cowton, the curator of the Wordsworth collection, for his encouragement. The portrait of William Wordsworth by Henry Edridge used on the front cover of the book is reproduced with the permission of the Wordsworth Trust. I am also grateful to James Crowden, Peter Frost-Pennington and the Catholic Study Circle for Animal Welfare for poems resulting from the 2001 outbreak of Foot and Mouth Disease in Cumbria.

The preparation of this book for publication would not have been possible without the invaluable help of my friend, Thania Wilcox. I am indebted to her for her technical advice and continuous encouragement.

Finally I acknowledge the contribution of my wife, Jenny, who has shared so many experiences with me in the Lake District over many years, dating from our first visit in 1979 with our children, who also love the area.

The book is dedicated to all who love the poetry of William Wordsworth and enjoy the serenity of the Lake District landscape.

Contents

Chapter 1 Beginnings 1
Chapter 2 Personal Landscapes 7
                Infinite Variety 11
                Light and Shade 13
                Autumn Glory 14
                Cultural Heritage 15
                A Sense of Wonder 16
                Points of View: 19
                *The Gaia Hypothesis 20
Chapter 3 Wordsworth and His Times 21
                Railway: Friend or Foe? 23
Chapter 4 Fearful landscapes 31
                The Beautiful and the Sublime 40
                Thoughts on *Mountain Gloom and Mountain Glory* ... 42
Chapter 5 In search of the spiritual 53
                Natural Science or Natural Theology 63
                Then and Now: Our Wordsworthian Heritage 66
                The Bible and Environmental Issues 68
                      OLD TESTAMENT 72
                      NEW TESTAMENT 73
                BBC Reith Lectures 2000 75
Chapter 6 Wordsworth and the Bliss of Solitude 79

	A Digression	86
	Back to the Lake District	93
Chapter 7	The Lake District and the Spirit of Place	97
	Place, Landscape and Imagination in the Poetry of William Wordsworth	102
	"Michael, A Pastoral Poem"	102
	"Fidelity"	107
	Easedale Beck and Easedale Tarn	109
	"Ode: The Pass of Kirkstone"	111
	Dungeon Ghyll and the Langdales	116
	Borrowdale	119
	Wordsworth and Picturesque Landscape	120
Chapter 8	Lordly and Majestic Duddon	125
	Sonnet 1	127
	Sonnet 2	127
	Sonnet 3	128
	Sonnets 4 and 5	128
	Sonnet 6 (Flowers)	129
	Sonnets 7 and 8	129
	Sonnet 9 (The Stepping-Stones)	130
	Sonnets 11 and 12	131
	Sonnets 13 (Open Prospect) and 14	131
	Sonnets 15, 16 (American Tradition) and 17 (Return)	132
	Sonnet 18. (Seathwaite Chapel)	134
	Sonnet 19 (Tributary Stream)	135
	Sonnet 20 (The plain of Donnerdale)	136
	Sonnet 21	137

Sonnet 22 (Tradition)	138
Sonnet 23 (Sheep-Washing)	138
Sonnet 24 (The Resting Place)	138
Sonnet 25	139
Sonnet 34 (After-Thought)	141
Chapter 9 Another Cumbrian Poet	143
Skiddaw Slate	149
Scafell Ash	150
Coniston Flag	152
Eskdale Granite	152
Mountain Limestone	153
Maryport Coal	154
St. Bees Sandstone	155
Chapter 10 National Parks: The Wilderness Experience	161
Environmental Values and Landscapes	167
Can "Wilderness" Be Defined	169
Chapter 11 Past, Present and Future	175
Forestry in the Lake District National Park	176
Wild Ennerdale	179
Hill Farming and the Conservation of the Landscape	182
Cumbrian Hill Farming: Marginal or Lost?	184
Poetry from the Crisis	185
Cumbria's Farming Landscape	189
A Geographical Diversion	190
Landforms	190
Climate	191

Chapter 12 A Special Place and Our Heritage 197
      "An eye to perceive and a heart to enjoy" 201
Epilogue 205
References 215

Chapter 1
Beginnings

The first visit to a place can often create an impression that lasts long in the memory. An unfavourable impression may last for a long time and prevent any wish to return. However, where the impression of a first visit is favourable, then it lasts in the memory and will be the inspiration for future visits. Although I had studied some of the geography of the area and was familiar with the poetry of William Wordsworth, I visited the Lake District for the first time at Easter 1979 when I was thirty-seven years old, my son fourteen and my daughter twelve. My wife and I decided to rent a small flat in the village of Lorton.

As with so many people of my generation the appeal of Mediterranean beaches and warm water and sunshine had taken us to the south of France, Spain and Portugal. We look back on visits to the Algarve before it was developed to the point that it resembles the worst excesses of the Spanish "Costa" resorts. Some years the appeal was the mountain landscapes of Austria and Switzerland, whereas other years our family holiday was spent in Brittany. Our preferred family accommodation was usually a villa or a *gite* and we avoided package holidays. These holiday destinations were and are preferred by many families and it seldom occurred to us to holiday in England. As I lived, and still do, in Dorset, we felt that we experienced the best England can offer in terms of coast and countryside throughout the year, and it was, therefore, sensible to have our summer holiday in Europe. Two holidays had been spent in Scotland and one in Pembrokeshire, but northern England was an unknown country. How wrong can anyone be to ignore some of the finest scenery in the United Kingdom?

The meagre knowledge I had of the Lake District was confined to the study of glaciation and radial drainage for Advanced Level Geography at a grammar school in Beckenham in the 1950s. Similarly, I had developed a love of the poetry of William Wordsworth in a course on the Romantic poets. The "Lyrical Ballads" made a lasting impression that is undiminished with the passing of the years. So it was at Easter 1979 that, as a family, we made our first visit to the Lake District and started what soon became a regular feature of each year. In the Vale of Lorton, it was natural that our first day in the area should be spent along the road to Crummock Water and eventually to Buttermere. I shall never forget the first view of Crummock Water, still and deserted on that spring morning, seen across sloping fields, bracken and heather with a herd of highland cattle in the foreground. It was a Sunday morning and the sky was clear and yet the chill of early morning gave freshness to the air. We felt the silence of that first view and from that moment, I have enjoyed so much peace of mind and serenity of spirit in this wonderful landscape.

Since that day I have made so many visits to the Vale of Lorton, and I hardly ever visit the area without walking the circuit of Buttermere. It is, for me, the most beautiful of all the lakes, surrounded by mountains and open fell. I never tire of Buttermere, whichever way it is walked, in every season of the year. As with so many places in the Lake District, every visit reveals something new, whatever the season or the weather on the day. However, to talk of favourite lakes is perhaps unnecessary. A walk around other lakes and tarns brings out similar feelings. It is perhaps not a question of which lake is the most beautiful but rather a complex web of emotions brought to life by the beauty of the Lakeland landscape.

The inspiration for this book comes from several different influences and is really the result of many visits and experiences. The book is an attempt to examine the environment and the landscape of place, principally in the Lake District, and the poetry of William Wordsworth is at the heart of every chapter. It is argued that our view of landscape has much to do with culture, aesthetics and history, as well as wider spiritual issues, always remembering that landscape appreciation is a very personal response to place. In the widest sense, our environmental appreciation is the result of the values we hold, and it seems to me, that several statements of intent should underpin our environmental values. These statements are not the only responses to landscape and some are, inevitably subjective, but they may find a response in a reader's mind and their attitude to the environment and the spirit of place:

- To accept our responsibility to maintain a sustainable environment for future generations: a key to this aim is to be found in the concept of *stewardship*, that accepts that we have a responsibility towards our environment, that is unique to human beings,
- To understand the place of human beings within nature and our ability to change or modify the environment for good or ill,
- To understand our responsibilities towards other species,
- To ensure that development can be justified and is appropriate to each locality,
- To preserve balance and diversity in nature wherever possible,
- To preserve areas of beauty and interest for future generations,
- To repair, wherever possible, a habitat damaged by human development and other causes.

Such aims are all embracing, and it is not always possible to keep them in balance. The aims and objectives of all environmental management are, however, clear. If the reader notices an underlying emphasis on *greenness* in our view of landscape, then the author makes no apology. It will be argued that a *green* view of landscape is present in much of the poetry of the Romantic era, particularly in the writings of William Wordsworth. An awareness of green issues goes hand in hand with the view that landscape appreciation can be seen in an aesthetic of place, even a spiritual view of the natural world.

In perhaps unintended ways, I am sure my background in education will surface from time to time in this book. I have found that one of the failings of modern education is that generations of children have received an education that is *subject-based* or even *subject-dominated*. Too often it is assumed that students will make connections between studies in different subjects. The reality is more likely to be that students make no such connections and simply reinforce the compartmental approach to education. An appreciation of landscape and place brings together many different strands of learning and experience, truly an interdisciplinary approach.

To use an educational analogy, Geography has always been seen as an integrating subject, a bridge between the arts and sciences with the possibility of links across the curriculum. Such links need not be artificial or contrived and can be exciting and intellectually rewarding. Patrick Bailey (1980) in a discussion paper on links between Geography and Religious Education wrote of the ethical aspects of geography and concluded:

> One of its central concepts is with the present condition of man in the world; and because that condition is profoundly affected by man's view of himself and of his fellow man, and those views depend very much upon his ideas of God, or his belief that God does not exist, the geographer and the student of religions have much in common to discuss. The detailed exploration of what this means for the development of linked and integrated teaching in schools has yet to be seriously undertaken.[1]

I have no doubt that my first view of Crummock Water and Buttermere has remained in my memory and the experience of that first morning returns every time my wife and I visit the valley. Memories of our young children are perhaps uppermost in our minds, but there is so much that floods into my mind every time I see the first view of Crummock Water. In the stillness of an early spring day with few people and even fewer cars on the road, it is possible to hear bird song and the bleat of sheep; nearer the lakeside there is the gentle lap of the water on a deserted shoreline. Surely, no one can be unmoved by such a sight, and for the Christian, the experience speaks of the renewal of life after a long winter and the freshness of the resurrection morning. The landscape speaks to us, and if we do not hear the words, then something is missing from our lives. The memories of that first morning by Crummock Water are fresh in my mind as I hear my grandchildren speak of the picnics they have enjoyed beside the same streams and paths, travelled by their grandfather back in the spring of 1979. Such is the power of memory and the closeness of the generations, inspired by the same location and overawed by the same landscape.

A fine example of the way we should view landscape and place is to be found in the 2005 BBC Television series, *A Picture of Britain*[2] where landscape is viewed through the eyes of poets and painters, farmers and rural workers, historians, tourists and musicians. The pattern was established in the first programme of the series on "The Romantic North" and a reviewer has noted that "Wordsworth's poetry invested landscape with deep spiritual meaning, and he admired art that did the same." It is true that poets and painters often interpret a landscape in ways that are not a true representation of reality, but in so many ways this helps us to understand the essential spirit of place. The reviewer went on to comment on this fact of artistic licence:

> That artists were interpreting and re-imaging their subject matter was, of course, not unique to the landscape genre, but by doing so they were influencing, even inventing, Britain's own image of itself, the personality ascribed to its very geography.[3]

One more reference to education illustrates the way in which landscape should be viewed in a holistic way. David W. Jardine (1997)[4] in writing of the integrated curriculum expressed, in a very poetic way, a view of learning that resonates throughout this book:

> I like to walk alone on country paths, rice plants and wild grasses on both sides, putting each foot down on the earth in mindfulness, knowing that I walk on the wondrous earth. In such moments, existence is…miraculous and mysterious. People usually consider walking on water or in thin air a miracle. But I think the real miracle is . . . to walk on earth. Every day we are engaged in a miracle which we don't even recognise: a blue sky, white clouds, green leaves, the black, curious eyes of a child. All is miracle.

In this view of life on earth as a miracle, the author is surely expressing truths that underpin all learning experiences; it is a statement expressing a sense of wonder in all we see and experience. Later in the same chapter there is a telling statement concerning curricular knowledge:

> Curricular knowledge is not all we give to our children; the really important skill or knowledge is their ability to live, their ability to be on Earth that will sustain their lives. It is possible to put a boundary around a subject and not see that a subject has an application to our lives and the life of the Earth. Subject boundaries can be seen as a means of keeping other people (other interpretations, other understandings) out.[5]

As I travel throughout the Lake District, I see people of all ages enjoying the peace and beauty of landscape. In a day's walk I may see several school parties engaged in an environmental or geomorphological study. It brings back to my mind the many young people I have introduced to the area and the experiences we have enjoyed. It has always been my wish that these young people become aware of the beauty around them and truly experience a tranquil sense of place. The same walk may pass parents with very young children, all hoping to give their sons and daughters a first experience of natural landscape that will remain with them all their lives. As well as these younger visitors, there are always those who have seen it all before; those who look back on happy memories of place and circumstance, who remember, as I do, their first visit to the Lake District and their first experience of the awe-inspiring wonder of the natural world.

This book is dedicated to those who love landscape and poetry, who appreciate the spirit of place and experience in nature a sense of wonder. We will look at some of Wordsworth's greatest poetry. We will examine some of the issues facing landowners and environmentalists and the need for conservation in the twenty-first century. We will also look at some of the environmental values expressed in the Old and New Testament, in recognition of the fact that there is a spiritual dimension to our appreciation of nature and the natural world. As our view of landscape and place is partly the result of cultural and aesthetic values, an attempt is made to examine the way we view mountains and wilderness scenery. Landscape is an inter-disciplinary experience, and it is that experience which is the theme and rationale of this book.

> *The heavens declare the glory of God;*
> *and the firmament sheweth*
> *His handiwork. (Psalm 19:1)*

Chapter 2
Personal Landscapes

If beauty is in the eye of the beholder, then an appreciation of landscape is equally subjective, to the point that two people may respond to a particular landscape in different ways. There may be similarities between the perceptions of two people but differences may still exist in an individual's appreciation of a landscape or a sense of place.

Some of the differences in the appreciation of landscape may be cultural and may change over time or with the age of the one who observes. Before the Romantic era of the last years of the eighteenth century and the first half of the nineteenth century many, perhaps most people, viewed mountain landscapes as hostile, remote, untamed and frightening places, where the human scale was dwarfed by wild nature. After the Romantic era the remoteness and wildness of mountains remained but the perception of many people was quite changed. In the words of Marjorie Hope Nicolson (1959)[1] an author mentioned extensively in this book, the aesthetics of mountain landscapes changed during the Romantic era and such landscapes were viewed, not as places of unrelieved gloom but places where we can experience the glories of nature. In terms of landscape appreciation, this change in people's perception of 'wild' landscape was one of the most dramatic changes emanating from the Romantic era in poetry, literature and art.

It can be argued that landscape appreciation is primarily the result of a subjective, intensely personal view of a place or region. We create a landscape in the mind that influences the way we view a place. Such a view is the result of many previous thought processes, some of which may be the unconscious memory of previous experiences. We may, for example, have nostalgic memories of childhood holiday visits to the countryside. These memories can be a positive or negative stimulus to our appreciation of any landscape. If we remember a beach holiday in Devon or Cornwall, when we enjoyed unbroken sunshine, then we may react very positively to coastal landscapes. In contrast, if we remember a holiday in the Lake District or Snowdonia when it rained every day, then we may have a more negative view of such landscapes. In reality, of course, the vagaries of weather apply to every type of landscape or place.

If landscape appreciation is personal and individual, then the same landscape can be viewed with very different emotions dependent upon the viewer's perspective. A tourist in the Lake District for a walking holiday may see the fells and mountains as places where wildness and solitude are the overwhelming attractions. In contrast, a hill farmer trying to make a living from his two or three hundred sheep and a few suckling calves may see each day as a struggle, in such marginal farming landscapes. The tourist may enjoy a walk in idyllic countryside whereas the farmer may see the same countryside as a landscape to be endured in an effort to survive. In many ways the farming landscape that is so attractive to the tourist is the result of generations of farmers working the land for meagre returns, and this way of thinking has been to the fore in the debate on farming in the National Parks, where farmers are increasingly seen as custodians of the landscape, with the need to be financially rewarded for their role in conservation.

One thing that has to be remembered in any discussion of landscape appreciation is the powerful influence of cultural influences on the individual. It is no exaggeration to say that rural areas and areas of rugged hills and valleys have become incorporated into what can loosely be called the 'Heritage' industry. As the population has become more and more urbanised the countryside has increasingly been seen as a place of recreation and escape. Nostalgia is a powerful influence on the way we look at rural areas and is not always a characteristic feeling of only the older members of society.

Unfortunately a longing for the past, and a wistful looking back at the landscape and rural life of earlier generations, can result in a sentimental idealization of countryside, seen in the sunlight of a golden age that almost certainly never existed. Such a view is not limited to rural areas. The popularity of open-air museums such as Blists Hill Victorian Town and other heritage sites in the Ironbridge area, or the Black Country Living Museum at Dudley, may result in a mixture of emotions in the minds of visitors.

There is no doubt that these living museums are a powerful stimulus to historical understanding, not just by children but also for all generations. The reconstructed buildings and the fact that we can see and talk to people in period dress, who perform tasks and act out life during the Industrial Revolution, has transformed the view of the past and the study of history. However, it is possible to come away from such sites with a *sanitised* view of the past without any real appreciation of the unremitting struggle of life in industrial cities. Perhaps such visits should be compared to the life of people described in Elizabeth Gaskell's *North and South* or Charles Dickens' *Hard Times*. Alternatively, visits to such locations can engender patriotic feelings, that we have lost something of great value, in that the United Kingdom is no longer the *workshop* of the world.

Similarly, those who live in urban areas may have a view of life in the countryside, either today or in the past, which is misleading and lacks understanding. As we have become an increasingly urban and suburban society, there is a danger that we may idealize the unity between man and his environment or we lose an understanding of the interdependence between the environment and ourselves. At a superficial level this trend may be seen in the fact that rural life is seen as quaint or old fashioned or, that young children may think that milk is made in a factory by the supermarket. A more serious lack of understanding is that farmland is viewed as simply a place of recreation. It can be argued that such a misunderstanding, at its most extreme, leads to a lack of awareness, by many in urban areas, of the seriousness of the 2001 outbreak of Foot and Mouth disease; it may even have been the cause of some of the arguments and prejudices behind the campaign to ban hunting with dogs.

These issues concern our perception of the past and the present, but there are other things that influence our view of landscape. One of the aims of this book is to explore the way we view landscape. There is no doubt that it is possible to have a scientific vision of nature and to view landscape in geological or ecological terms. In some ways our appreciation of nature is heightened if we understand the morphology of landscape or the interdependence of flora and fauna. However, it is possible to have an imaginative vision of any landscape and this book is an attempt to view the Lake District in such a way, particularly through the eyes of poets.

It is, perhaps, a truism to say that different things appeal to different people and this, of course, explains why some people are attracted to particular landscapes and others see little of beauty, meriting many return visits. Marion Shoard[2] (1982) attempted to analyse the appeal of semi-wild and wilderness areas and her conclusions are mentioned later in this book. It is personally rewarding, for everyone, to think about what makes a landscape attractive or otherwise, to develop a personal analysis of landscape appreciation. I have done this for many different rural landscapes and no more so than in the Lake District. Many of my preferences are revealed throughout this book but here it may be useful to list facets of the Lakeland landscape which are particularly attractive to my eyes and which combine to form my appreciation of this unique landscape. Such an exercise is recommended for the reader of these very personal values.

My personal view of the Lake District is largely determined by a consideration of five interrelated visions that appeal to my sense of well-being and enjoyment of this precious landscape; they can be summarised as:

- Infinite Variety,
- Light and Shade,
- Autumn Glory,
- Cultural Heritage,
- A Sense of Wonder.

It is appreciated that these five ways of looking at the region may not resonate with all readers and they are by no means all inclusive. It is, however, hoped that others will examine their own appreciation of landscape and that the process will lead to a deepening love and respect for our natural heritage.

Infinite Variety

It is possible in a few days in the Lake District to experience a greater variety of landscapes than almost anywhere else in the United Kingdom. Even in a day's rambling we can go from the seclusion of the Duddon valley to the grandeur of the Wrynose Pass. The silence of Buttermere and Crummock Water is intensified by the towering slopes on each side of the valley and yet, as you leave Crummock Water towards the Vale of Lorton the fertile fields give the impression of ordered calm as the mountains to the south recede and become a backcloth to a pastoral scene.

In the shaded depths at the entrance to the Borrowdale valley, with a vertical cliff to one side, it is difficult to imagine that above is Ashness Bridge and the hidden valley of Watendlath, the two locations linked by the Cataract of Lodore.

An even greater variety of landscape and location is to be found on either side of Ullswater. Along the western shore is the A 592 linking the tourist honey pots of Pooley Bridge and Aira Force to the villages of Glenridding and Patterdale. In contrast, on the eastern shore is the hamlet of Howtown, with its landing stage for the Ullswater launches. Taking the road beyond Howtown, in a series of hairpin bends, we find the isolated valley of Martindale, with its herd of red deer and small farms, leading eventually to the path up to High Street with memories of the Roman legions making their way to Hadrians Wall. Similarly, the equally isolated valleys of Boredale and Fusedale, make it possible to enjoy the peace and silence of these locations. One of the truly great lowland walks of the Lake District extends from Howtown to Patterdale. In the space of a few hours walking we go from the relative isolation and quietness of Howtown to the welcome hospitality of the tearooms at Side Farm and the small settlement of Patterdale, taking in wonderful views of the lake and the mountains and fells beyond, leading up to the summit of Helvellyn.

The whole area is full of contrasting landscapes, and some appeal to one person but not to another. Even on a single farm we find astonishing variety, from the valley floor inbye fields to the slopes of the intake and the rugged stone walls, with the vastness of the open fell roamed by Herdwick sheep; on a single farm we move from secure fold to wild fell. It is this variety that makes the Lake District so appealing.

Another facet of the infinite variety of the Lake District landscape concerns the flow of water, as it reflects the changing seasons and the interplay of slope and landscape. At one extreme we have the variety of waterfalls, from the wooded cascades of Aira Force to the open water of Scale Force into Buttermere and the stepped falls into the Seathwaite valley in Borrowdale. At the other extreme we have the infinite variety of stream flow that is such a feature of any part of Lakeland.

The flow of water is but one aspect of the infinite variety of landscape in the region. William Wordsworth in his "Tintern Abbey" poem wrote: "The sounding cataract haunted me like a passion…"

This poem was set in the Wye Valley but how easily this thought can be transferred to the flow of water in the Lake District. In the course of any walk in the area we are never far from the sound of water. Simply sitting by any stream, in any valley of the region, we can experience every register of the music of landscape. We hear the gentle, high-pitched sound of water flowing over the rock and pebbles of a mountain stream, the sounds of the flute and piccolo, and yet, even within a few yards, we hear the more guttural, throaty sounds of a stream with a purpose, a stream making a more determined effort to reach flatter land.

In 1935, the Chinese artist and poet, Chiang Yee, visited several parts of the Lake District and recorded the experience in a book, *The Silent Traveller—A Chinese Artist in Lakeland*. In a walk in Lanthwaite Woods, he observed the river flowing from Crummock Water and thought of how another Chinese poet described the sound of running water:

> There are many types of the sound of running water —
> that of water falling, of flowing into the distance, of
> swirling or billowing, of breaking on rocks, of lakes, of
> rivers, of streams, and so on; one could choose to listen to
> any of these, and one's mood might be altered in
> accordance with it. There the sound of the small running
> stream I heard what might have been one of his types — it

was like a pair of lovers whispering and laughing under the trees with lowered voices; their words were not audible, but had they been the happy chatterers would never have cared.[3]

If the sounds of water, flowing in so many different ways, are coupled with the other sounds of landscape, particularly the voices of wind as they pass through grass and heather, bracken and woodland, across open water and sheltered tarn, through deep forest and open fell, we come closer to understanding the beauty of nature and the sublime sound of the infinite.

Light and Shade

The infinite variety of Lakeland scenery greatly enhances the feeling and experience of the changing light of the area, especially when the sun is shining and the skies are blue. We can in the space of an hour move from sunlit lakes and sparkling streams to the darkness of a conifer forest and the dappled sunlight of deciduous woodland. In spring and early summer, many of the woodlands are enriched by clumps of daffodils, that give way to a carpet of bluebells, and all is overhung by fresh green leaves as trees are once again resurrected to the new life of another year of growth and vitality. We associate bluebells with deciduous woodland but at Rannerdale on the eastern side of Crummock Water there is a vast expanse of bluebells on open land. After flowering, the bluebell plants become sheltered by the growth of bracken, that mimics the effect of deciduous woodland.

In autumn and winter there is a similar interplay of light and shade, ranging from the cold sunlight on mountain peaks and valley sides to the enduring shade of the deepest valleys or the snow-capped summits and hoar frost of sheltered valleys. Even the ragged curtains of mist and rain over the bleak winter fells are not without their austere and threatening beauty.

Sitting by a lakeside reveals another example of light and shade. The surface of the water changes minute by minute and reflects the sunlight and the effects of wind upon a water surface. I am reminded of a morning in spring when seated a little above Crummock Water. A strong breeze was blowing from the southwest producing patterns on the surface of the lake. As a stronger breeze flowed across the lake, if only for a minute or so, the water was ruffled and displayed a darker water surface that could be followed across the lake. Similarly, the reflection of the sun and the clouds on the surface of water can lead to rapidly changing views of landscape and place. In the space of a few minutes the lake surface, especially on a still day, can change from a mirror like image to a broken and darker reflection of trees and mountains. It is the same when clouds are seen to pass a shadow across valley sides and landscapes showing how fast the clouds are moving. Such contrasts are not unique to the Lakes but are one of the enduring memories of the landscape. The light and shade in nature never ceases to impress and is part of the feeling of awe and wonder of the natural world.

An example of light and shade is found in Dorothy Wordsworth's journal entry for December 26, 1801. Wordsworth and his sister set out on a walk to Rydal and as they passed Grasmere Lake she was impressed by the stillness of the water and its reflections:

> It was very pleasant—Grasmere Lake a beautiful image of stillness, clear as glass, reflecting all things, the wind was up, and the waters sounding. The lake of a rich purple, the fields a soft yellow, the island yellowish-green, the copses red-brown, the mountains purple. The Church and buildings, how quiet they were!

Autumn Glory

As the days shorten and nature hangs on to the last warmth of Summer, many areas of the Lake District display a kaleidoscope of colour; not perhaps the "season of mist and mellow fruitfulness" of lowland areas but a glorious mix of reds and rusts, deepening greens and chestnut browns of valley-side bracken. The fiery larches mingle with the racing-green pines and woodlands, where just a few months earlier there were carpets of lemon green daffodils and royal blue bluebells. In autumn we find a carpet of multi-coloured leaves. As one walker said to me recently, "Who needs Vermont when we've got Lakeland?" In these days of global warming, heavy frosts, especially hoar frost are perhaps rarer events, but when they coincide with the autumnal colours at their best, the landscape is transformed into a magical fairy land, where all the golden brown and russet leaves glisten as if covered with a myriad of tiny lights. Some people see autumn as the beginning of winter heralding darker days and lower temperatures and, of course, this is true; however, others see the season as the crowning glory at the end of summer.

Cultural Heritage

Some areas of the country are able to speak to us of great moments in British history, where the links with the past are obvious to all and the past comes alive in a variety of buildings, ranging from castles and palaces to manor houses, country churches and ancient ruins. In the Lake District the cultural heritage is just as great in most of these respects but there are added cultural associations unique to the area.

In so much of the Lake District we walk in the steps of William Wordsworth, his sister Dorothy and other literary personalities such as Samuel Taylor Coleridge, Robert Southey and John Ruskin. The presence of Wordsworth is felt in a walk around Grasmere, Rydal Water and Loughrigg Terrace. We can in our mind's eye see him walking in John's Wood at Grasmere, as he talks to his seafaring brother, John. His "Duddon" sonnets make a walk in this quiet, isolated valley even more enjoyable and who can walk in Gowbarrow woods, at Wordsworth Point beside Ullswater and not be inspired by that "host of dancing daffodils"?

Other literary figures crowd in on the imagination and give a special sense of place to other locations. John Ruskin's Brantwood with its commanding views over Coniston Water and the Old Man of Coniston standing supreme on the western side of the lake; we can walk with Norman Nicholson as we read his descriptions of Lakeland life and read his poetry; Peter Rabbit, Jemima Puddleduck and Squirrel Nutkin can still be seen in Mr McGregor's garden at Hill Top; and no walk around Buttermere is complete without the hope of a glimpse of Mary Robinson, the Maid of Buttermere.

There are so many other echoes from the past in this delightful area, which remind us of past achievements and initiatives. The birth of the National Trust is commemorated at Friar's Crag on Derwentwater and some of the finest scenery and locations in the Lake District are conserved for future generations by this great national institution. The creation of the Lake District National Park in 1951 was a landmark date ensuring that the area will be preserved and conserved for future generations. No visitor to Coniston can fail to think of Donald Campbell and his fatal attempt, in "Bluebird" to achieve a water speed record on Coniston Water.

One of the themes of this book is the change in people's perception and appreciation of mountain scenery and here in the Lake District we get nearer than anywhere else in England, to seeing the transition from "Mountain Gloom" to "Mountain Glory," largely but not exclusively, the result of the influence of the writers of the Romantic era.

The industrial heritage of the area is not as obvious as in other areas of the country but it is there none the less. We can visit the many sites of past mining and quarrying, one of the most spectacular being Honister Mines and Quarries, with the opportunity to enter the mines and view their working. Even in the Duddon Valley, one of the quieter areas of the region, there are memories of a cottage industry for spinning and weaving and the remains of several Bobbin mills. The arrival of the railway at Windermere was an enormous boost to the tourist industry, in spite of Wordsworth's opposition!

One other aspect of our cultural heritage is to be seen all over the Lake District in the ever present Herdwick sheep, hefted flocks which add to the appeal of the area to thousands of tourists. The contribution of farmers to the preservation of the landscape cannot be exaggerated, their work only reaching the headlines when disaster strikes as in the 2001 Foot and Mouth outbreak. During those months of disaster for the farmers of the Lakes, there was an eerie silence throughout much of the region, not the silence of contemplation but a silence reflecting the loss of livelihood and a growing sense of despair. The landscape looked the same but an essential element was missing.

A Sense of Wonder

This is an intensely personal appreciation of the Lake District and others may approach their own landscape analysis in different ways. It is obviously the case that different things appeal to different people, although there are probably many facets of the area that appeal equally to a large number of visitors and residents.

The Lake District never fails to please me at all seasons and in all weathers. It is a place where I can feel close to the natural world, a place for contemplation and somewhere to experience all that is good about England. Even though parts of the area can be busy, crowded and noisy, there are still so many places where one can feel away from it all. At its best the area gives an opportunity to listen to the natural world and to listen to the sound of silence.

As William Wordsworth mused on the feelings experienced on seeing once again the fields and woods of the Wye valley, he came to a profound conclusion which many feel in the open air and in the midst of special landscapes; emotions that touch the heart but enter into the deepest recesses of the soul:

> *For I have learned*
> *To look on nature, not as in the hour*
> *Of thoughtless youth; but hearing oftentimes*
> *The still sad music of humanity,*
> *Not harsh nor grating, though of ample power*
> *To chasten and subdue. And I have felt*
> *A presence that disturbs me with the joy*
> *Of elevated thoughts; a sense sublime*
> *Of something far more deeply interfused,*
> *Whose dwelling is the light of setting suns,*
> *And the round ocean, and the living air,*
> *And the blue sky, and in the mind of man,*
> *A motion and a spirit, that impels*
> *All thinking things, all objects of all thought,*
> *And rolls through all things.*
> *(Lines Written a Few Miles above Tintern Abbey, on*
> *Revisiting the Banks of the Wye during a Tour, July 13,*
> *1798 Lines 89–103)*

There is something of the spiritual about all such areas and it brings me to an awareness of the beauty of the world about us, which is special and can be experienced in a single flower or the grandest landscapes. Even though the planet has been polluted in so many ways and mankind has abused the natural world through ignorance and worse, there are still so many places where the human spirit is uplifted and we can appreciate that we are so small and insignificant in the greater scheme of things. To the Christian, these thoughts were expressed so eloquently by the writer of Psalm 104, which one writer has said is an example of "Natural Religion," the whole Psalm seeing the phenomena of nature as the work of God:

> *O Lord, how manifold are Thy works! In wisdom hast Thou made them all: The earth is full of Thy riches. (Psalm 104:24)*[4]

These five facets of landscape are intensely personal and have influenced my view of landscape over many years. They may, in their interaction with each other, be entirely personal, although I suspect others will find them to be part of their own vision of landscape. In the course of a career in teaching, lesson notes and plans accumulate in dusty files, some perhaps never again to see the light of day! However, in writing this book, certain themes have emerged from past teaching, which have a bearing on the issues raised in several chapters. As well as explaining some of my approaches to landscape appreciation, they also exhibit certain values and attitudes concerning our responsibility towards the environment.

In Chapter 1, the dominance of the subject curriculum in secondary education, experienced by most readers, was mentioned and a case made for attempts to cross subject boundaries. In looking at the geography curriculum over many years, I have noticed that students are rarely asked to consider some of the views on the environment held by some of the world's religions. Similarly, in Religious Education students are rarely asked to consider the impact of religion and culture on some of the environmental issues of concern in the world today? Why is it that a geographical study of the Lake District is unlikely to include a consideration of Norman Nicholson's poem "The Seven Rocks," a study of the seven main rocks of the area?[5]

If we are able to look at the environment in a spiritual way, which perhaps leads to an acceptance that we have a duty of stewardship, should we not be aware of the beliefs and values of Christians and Jews, Muslims, Hindus and Buddhists? Is it realistic to assume that all the world's faiths have the same outlook on the environment? Is there any connection between the impact of beliefs and values and the economic circumstances of a nation or group of peoples? Are believers in an economically less developed country likely to view the environment in a way significantly different to believers in an economically more developed country? These are questions that are difficult to answer but should they not be addressed?

One very effective way of examining our perspective on environmental issues is to examine the views of people from different backgrounds and times. In each case a series of questions should be asked:

- What is each person saying about the environment?
- What does each statement say about that person's beliefs and values?
- Does each statement say something important about our response to the many environmental issues facing us today?
- If the world took notice of each of the statements, would it make a difference for good?

Points of View:

"We do not inherit the earth from our parents; we borrow it from our children." (North American Indian)

"When we respect the environment, then nature is good to us. When our hearts are good, then the sky will be good to us. The trees are like our mother and father, they feed us, nourish us, and provide us with everything; fruit, leaves, the branches, the trunk. They give us food and satisfy our needs." (Buddhist monk)

"The exploration of outer space takes place at the same time as the earth's own oceans, seas, and fresh water areas grow increasingly polluted. Many of the earth's habitats, animals, plants, insects, and even micro-organisms that we know are rare may not be known at all by future generations. We have the capability and the responsibility. We must act before it is too late." (The Dalai Lama)

"We are not managers or masters of the Earth, we are just workers chosen by the others, the rest of life on the planet." (James Lovelock—who propounded the Gaia hypothesis* of the biosphere)

"The end of man's creation was that he should be God's steward. Man was endowed with this dominion, trust and care...to preserve the face of the earth in beauty, usefulness and fruitfulness." (Sir Matthew Hale, in 1677)

> The kiss of the sun for pardon,
> The song of the birds for mirth,
> One is nearer God's heart in a garden
> Than anywhere else on earth.
> (Dorothy Gurney)

*The Gaia Hypothesis

The Gaia hypothesis was put forward in 1979 by the British scientist, James Lovelock.[6] The name comes from GAIA, who was the Greek goddess of the Earth. The hypothesis suggests that the biosphere is a self-regulating organism, able to react to damage, in a way that will bring about healing and restoration; in much the same way as the human body is able to restore equilibrium and allow wounds to heal.

The hypothesis is not accepted by many in the scientific community, although many people are attracted to it, for if the earth is seen in this way, it is argued that we may be more inclined to act more responsibly towards the environment. It has influenced some environmental groups, particularly Friends of the Earth. To see the earth as a super-organism may lead to questioning of the misuse of many ecosystems which carries with it unknown and possibly tragic results.

Even if much of the scientific community dismisses the Gaia Hypothesis, it is at the very least, a force for shaping values and attitudes, towards a more sustainable use of the earth's resources and ecosystems.

Chapter 3
Wordsworth and his times

William Wordsworth (1770-1850) lived during the first decades of the Industrial Revolution, when Britain changed in so many momentous ways; changes in the social structure of the nation, in the economic, technical and cultural life of the world's first industrial nation. Wordsworth was six years old when in 1776 the Americans first drafted the Declaration of Independence, heralding the beginning of the long decline of the British Empire. As a young man he travelled in France and Italy, including a significant walking tour in the Alps. Wordsworth was, as a young man, a passionate supporter of the French Revolution and had strong republican views. England's declaration of war against France in 1793 shocked him deeply, although following the excesses of the "Terror"[1] he became disillusioned with the politics of nations and retreated into a contemplation of the ideal certainties of nature.

In 1776, Adam Smith published his great and influential work, *An Inquiry into the Nature and Causes of the Wealth of Nations*. This book revolutionised the economic theories of the day and eventually led to factories and assembly line production. Several major technical advances occurred during Wordsworth's life, of which the most significant were the mechanisation of the textile industry; major developments in the use of coal and iron; the introduction of steam power and the growth of factories and industrial towns, a process of rapid urbanisation that has continued for much of the twentieth century and into the twenty-first century.

Wordsworth was also of the generation that saw a complete change in our view of landscape, particularly mountainous scenery. It is possible to argue that this was the time when our view of wilderness areas, even of nature itself, underwent a dramatic change. During his life, Wordsworth saw the first stirrings of a concern for natural landscapes that was to lead, eventually, to the birth of the National Trust and the creation of National Parks in this country and throughout the world. Parallel to these developments was the growth of industrial towns and cities, together with a growing difference between town and country. It did not matter that so much of the landscape of England was the result of farming practice over many centuries for the perception was that rural areas were natural whereas towns and cities were the result of the decisions of people.

In 1810, Wordsworth published anonymously his *Guide to the Lakes*, one of the first books of its kind, which was an immediate success, with five editions printed before the final version was published in 1835. It is to a large extent true to say that during Wordsworth's lifetime, the Lake District became a popular tourist attraction, perhaps to some extent, because of his guidebook. One of the enduring features of Wordsworth's guidebook is that it is still possible to use it today as a source of information on the attractions of the area. It is interesting to speculate on how Wordsworth would view the area today. Undoubtedly he would recognise the beauty of the fells and the quieter areas of the Lake District. The views around Crummock Water and Buttermere would still inspire him, even though farming has changed in the Lorton valley and the National Trust carefully manages the two lakesides. However, how would he feel about the development and popularity of such honey-pot locations as Bowness, Windermere and Ambleside? Even Grasmere today, with its many visitors and traffic, would surely not escape his critical eye? Would he be surprised that he is the centre of attraction in Grasmere and that the Wordsworth Centre with its collection of books, paintings and letters is a magnet for international visitors?

Wordsworth was concerned about some of the issues that still concern geographers and environmentalists, issues that are central to planning decisions for the future of the Lake District National Park and the wider area. He was aware of the effect on the landscape of the building of dams to create lakes as reservoirs, as was the case with Thirlmere; similarly, the planting of conifers without thought for the effect of such forests on the landscape. He was concerned about the impact of an increasing number of tourists, especially in summer months; in Wordsworth's day it was the coming of the railway to Windermere that was the main concern; today it is more likely to be road schemes or intrusive development in the National Park.

Even in Wordsworth's day there were conflicting arguments about the way in which the Lake District was becoming more accessible to larger numbers of people. These arguments centred on the coming of the railway to Windermere, which was seen as a threat to the whole area.

Railway: Friend or Foe?

The Kendal and Windermere Railway opened on the 21st April 1847 and the following year there was published 'Bradshaw's Railway and Steamer' timetable. This development made it possible for people living in Liverpool to visit Windermere on a week's excursion. For the first time, the Lake District became accessible to visitors on a short-term basis, as opposed to visitors who could afford to spend several months in the area.

It was a similar story that was repeated many times throughout the country during the nineteenth century, as railways made long distance travel possible for the mass of the population. Many seaside resorts in Southern England owe their development to the arrival of the railway.

Since the improvement in rail and road transport during the nineteenth century there have been different opinions on the impact of greater numbers of visitors to areas of attractive landscapes. One example from southern England illustrates these national trends. Even at the start of the twenty-first century, opposing views are being expressed as to the effect on the Isle of Purbeck in Dorset, particularly Corfe Castle and Studland, of an upgrading of the A351 to Wareham, allowing faster access from the Bournemouth/Poole conurbation. Unlike the Lake District, the Isle of Purbeck is not a National Park, but the pressure of tourist numbers in summer is likely to keep on increasing and this is as true of the Isle of Purbeck, as it is of the Lake District and other areas of natural beauty. This may be made more certain, in the Isle of Purbeck, now that the Dorset Jurassic coastline has been designated as a World Heritage Site. The same is true in many other areas of the United Kingdom. There is an enduring paradox that many areas, inside and outside the National

Parks, have become so popular that the sheer volume of visitors and traffic can destroy something of the beauty of an area.

In 1844, Wordsworth was strongly opposed to such an assault on an area he believed should be protected from mass tourism, although the concept was unknown to him at the time. His views were expressed in his sonnet, "On the Projected Kendal and Windermere Railway":

> *Is then no nook of English Ground secure*
> *From rash assault? Schemes of retirement sown*
> *In youth and 'mid the busy world kept pure*
> *As when the earliest flowers of hope were blown,*
> *Must perish:- how can they this blight endure?*
> *And must he too the ruthless change bemoan*
> *Who scorns a false utilitarian lure*
> *'Mid his paternal fields at random thrown?*
> *Baffle the threat, bright Scene, from Orrest-head*
> *Given to the pausing traveller's rapturous glance:*
> *Plead for thy peace, thou beautiful romance*
> *Of nature: and, if human hearts be dead,*
> *Speak, passing winds: ye torrents, with your strong*
> *And constant voice, protest against the wrong.*
> *October 12th 1844*

The strength of Wordsworth's feelings are clear in this sonnet, especially the use of words and phrases, "rash assault," "as when the earliest flowers of hope were blown, must perish," "the ruthless change bemoan" and "your strong and constant voice, protest against the wrong." The words, poetic as they are, have been repeated so many times, over the years, when treasured environments are under threat. Wordsworth's mention of "Orrest-head" refers to a favourite viewpoint, overlooking Lake Windermere; it is a hill north of Windermere town (G.R. 415994) and if visited by Wordsworth after the arrival of the railway in 1847, would have given him a clear view of the steam, as trains arrived at Windermere!

Wordsworth added a footnote to this sonnet, which goes some way to explain the strength of his feelings:

> Rydal Mount
> October 12th 1844
>
> The degree and kind of attachment which many of the yeomanry feel to their small inheritances can scarcely be overrated. Near the house of one of them stands a magnificent tree, which a neighbour of the owner advised him to fell for profit's sake; "Fell it" exclaimed the yeoman, "I had rather fall on my knees and worship it." It happens, I believe, that the intended railway would pass through this little property, and I hope that an apology for the answer will not be thought necessary by one who enters into the strength of the feeling.
>
> W.W.

Wordsworth sent his sonnet to the Editor of the Morning Post, a newspaper that was eventually to merge with the Daily Telegraph in 1937. He wrote two lengthy letters to the Morning Post in which he explained his reasons for being so opposed to the arrival of the railway in Windermere, to terminate at Bowness. Incidentally, he feared that the railway could eventually be extended to Ambleside and on to Grasmere, something that fortunately never happened.

Apart from the human need for railways to connect cities with other parts of the country, there were powerful economic reasons, for example, in reference to the local economy. The expansion of the railway network was often in response to the bulk transport of materials. However, in the Windermere district, Wordsworth argued that the quantity of manufactured goods was trifling; it had no mines and its quarries were either worked out or superseded by quarries in other areas. The soil is light and the cultivable parts of the country are very limited, so that it had little to send out and little had it also to receive. Such comments cannot always be accepted at face value and there is no doubt that Wordsworth had a distinct hidden agenda.

In Wordsworth's attitude to the arrival of the railway at Windermere, we have an example of how it can be 'proved', that a development is not necessary, by reference to economic facts, avoiding all charges that the writer is only concerned in preserving the status quo! Although Wordsworth accepted that summer tourists did visit the area, he did not see any connection between these few visitors and the need for a railway. He recognised that railways made long distance travel possible for many more people, but argued that it was sufficient to bring people to Kendal in the south, or to Penrith in the north; to enter farther into the Lakes was considered unnecessary. However, his fundamental objection was based on his belief that "artisans and labourers, and the humbler classes of shopkeepers should not be tempted to visit particular spots which they had not been educated to appreciate."

This comment sounds elitist and patronising by today's standards but it must be remembered that in the context of the mid-nineteenth century, Wordsworth's view of the majority of the population, living in the growing industrial towns and cities, was shared by many people of Wordsworth's background. However, it has to be said that Hartley Coleridge, the son of Wordsworth's friend, Samuel Taylor Coleridge, defended Wordsworth and said that he did not object to railways because they would bring a poorer class of people to the Lakes. Canon H.D. Rawnsley, in an address to the Wordsworth Society in 1883, quoted a letter written by Hartley Coleridge in which he said: "I believe Mr Wordsworth objects, not for himself, but for Nature and mankind."[2] To fully empathise with the attitudes and values of past societies can only be fully effective if there is a comprehensive understanding of society at the time. Many poets, artists and wealthy travellers were beginning to see wilder, more remote mountainous areas as very attractive, but for many, such areas were still too rugged, isolated, dangerous, even frightening landscapes.

The next chapter traces an aesthetic view of landscape during a period of great change, a view of mountainous areas that goes to the heart of the Romantic Movement.

There is one place in his two letters to the *Morning Post* where Wordsworth showed that he was not entirely elitist in wanting to prevent easier access to the Lake District. In arguing in favour of a Ten Hours Bill, with no reduction in wages and the necessities of life being available to all, Wordsworth wrote that "each individual would be at liberty to make at his own cost excursions in any direction which might be most inviting to him. There would then be no need for their masters sending them in droves scores of miles from their homes and families to the borders of Windermere, or anywhere else."[3] It is still possible to argue that his view was a clever way of saying that people were to be encouraged to travel anywhere, but hopefully not to the Lake District!

There was, however, an opposing voice to that of Wordsworth in 1845. In that year, he met Harriet Martineau (1802-1876), who came and settled in Ambleside. She was an influential writer on the Unitarian faith, as well as works on political economy and social affairs; she had travelled fairly extensively in America, in support of the abolition of slavery. Harriet Martineau did not share Wordsworth's exalted view of the Lake District's landscape and rather saw the area as a place for refreshment, "for people living in stench, huddled together in cabins, and almost without water." However, these conditions applied equally to dalesmen's families as to those in the industrial towns.

To her, the plan to extend the railway from Kendal to Bowness was welcomed for two reasons. First she saw that the area needed to be opened up to the rest of Northern England, so that new industries, trade and employment could alleviate the rural poverty of many in the Lakes. Her second reason was that the railway would make the area accessible to all the growing industrial towns of south Lancashire. In 1855 she published her *Complete Guide to the Lakes*[4] in which she appealed to the growing number of urban tourists who would benefit from the railway to Bowness.

Unlike Wordsworth, Harriet Martineau's guide is merely a description of routes and places, without any attempt to explore the spirit of place. Instead, she concentrated on the living conditions and way of life of the self-supporting statesmen, those at the poorest level of farming, where life was a constant drudgery and battle for survival. She noted the poor condition of many cottages and the land that surrounded them:

> The healthiness of many settlements is no less a shame
> than a curse, for the fault is in Man, not in Nature. Nature
> has fully done her part in providing rock for foundations,
> the purest air, and the amplest supply of running water;
> yet the people live—as we are apt to pity the poor of the

metropolis for living—in stench, huddled together in cabins, and almost without water. The wilfulness of this makes the fact almost incredible; but the fact is so.[5]

The difference in the view of these two writers appears to be irreconcilable. Wordsworth viewed man in a wider context. He viewed man in the landscape of the natural world, whereas Harriet Martineau saw people at the level of the living conditions of families. However, this may not be an accurate assessment of Wordsworth's understanding of the lives of many around him in the Lake District. An interesting commentary is to be found in Wordsworth's description of the living conditions of many of the statesmen farmers in the Lake District, as he expressed it in his pastoral poem, "Michael." He did not gloss over the hardship of Michael's daily struggle but neither did he concentrate on the details of the harsh conditions and the poverty of the shepherd's life. Wordsworth was more concerned with the nobility of this humble man's life and the romantic appreciation of such farming practices. He spoke of his first impression of Michael's life:

> *It was the first*
> *Of those domestic tales that spake to me*
> *Of Shepherds, dwellers in the valleys, men*
> *Whom I already loved; not verily*
> *For their own sakes, but for the fields and hills*
> *Where was their occupation and abode.*
> *And hence this Tale, while I was yet a Boy*
> *Careless of books, yet having felt the power*
> *Of Nature, by the gentle agency*
> *Of natural objects, led me on to feel*
> *For passions that were not my own, and think*
> *(At random and imperfectly indeed)*
> *On man, the heart of man, and human life.*
> *(Lines 21–33 of "Michael. A Pastoral Poem" 1800)*

Harriet Martineau wanted the arrival of the railway, whereas Wordsworth opposed it, and this fact illustrates the difference between the two characters. Harriet saw the opening up of the Lakes as the only hope for the poorest in society and she saw the outer world as a market for village trades. Wordsworth was more concerned about the effect of opening the area to the outside world on the landscape and character of the region. Both figures may have exaggerated their goals but there seems little doubt that future years would result in a merging and softening of these two conflicting views of the character of the Lake District.

In Canon H.D.Rawnsley's address to the Wordsworth Society in 1883 he spoke concerning the Proposed Permanent Lake District Defence Society, one of the forerunners of the National Trust. He commented on the battle that had been won over a proposed railway from Braithwaite to Buttermere and gave credit to Wordsworth who had opposed the railway reaching Windermere.[6]

He also quoted Professor John Stuart Blackie, who was Professor of Greek in the University of Edinburgh, and had spoken about the proposed railway in the strongest terms,

> *I cannot imagine any more sacred duty of good citizens, at the present moment, than to save the natural beauties of the country from the defacing operations of men who have no sense for anything in the world but mercantile speculation and the lust of gain. If God made the world beautiful, it was that its beauty might be enjoyed, and men have no right for local convenience and temporary utilities to make it systematically ugly.*[7]

Similarly, Sir Frederic Leighton who was President of the Royal Academy from 1878 to 1896 and was associated with the Pre-Raphaelites; he spoke with equal concern for the importance of conserving nature:

> *A passionate love for the beauties of Nature is one of the finest and most wholesome features of English character. The growing tendency to blot out or fail the springs from which that love is fed, is, in my view, a grave and forecasting evil.*[8]

Canon H.D.Rawnsley concluded his address to the Wordsworth Society with a call for vigilance:

> *Our only chance of keeping Lakeland inviolate is to be on the watch with a powerful national, one might dare to say international, committee. ... With a backing of Members*

> *of Parliament to help us at Westminster, and a considerable sum of money behind us for expenses if need be.*[9]

It is interesting to speculate how satisfied these nineteenth century worthies would be at the measures we have in place in the twenty-first century to conserve and preserve areas of natural beauty. Similarly, how will future generations look back on our efforts today?

Chapter 4
Fearful landscapes

In 1739 Horace Walpole, son of the Prime Minister Robert Walpole, toured the Alps with Thomas Gray, who was destined to be one of the most famous poets of the eighteenth century. His description of Borrowdale was to be an early inspiration for the young Wordsworth. In a bizarre incident in the Alps, when a wolf attacked and dragged away Walpole's King Charles spaniel, the two travellers saw the mountains as frightful and devilish places. Walpole wrote to Richard West and declared that "Mount Cenis, I confess, carries the permission mountains have of being frightful too far; and its horrors were accompanied with too much danger to give one time to reflect upon their beauties."[1] This is a graphic example of how we can react in fear to something that, at one and the same time, we find awe-inspiring and magnificent. The view that mountains are dangerous and frightful, and yet deserving of our reflection on their beauties, was a commonly held opinion in the pre-Romantic period.

For centuries mountains were seen as places of holy terror; the wildness of semi-wilderness landscapes was sufficient to make them landscapes of fear, to be avoided unless absolutely necessary. In reality, it is perhaps the wildness of all semi-wilderness, deserted areas, which caused people to avoid such landscapes. They were, for many centuries, perceived as frightening, threatening landscapes; mountains are merely the most extreme example of landscapes of fear. There are, however, other such landscapes of potential fear, such as deep and dark, impenetrable forests, lonely dry and desolate deserts, or the inhospitable landscapes of Polar latitudes.

One of the earliest English poems is *Beowulf*, which cannot be accurately dated but is generally supposed to date towards the end of the eighth century; much of the material in *Beowulf* is legendary and concerns the slaying of a monster, Grendel, and then Grendel's mother. The material may be legendary but the scenery around Grendel's home is described clearly enough, even though it cannot be located with any certainty. The reference to "perilous fen paths" perhaps suggests the Fens of East Anglia, although other landscapes described in the poem cannot be accurately identified:

> *A hidden valley they inhabit,*
> *Wolf-haunted valleys, perilous fen paths*
> *And windswept headlands, where the mountain stream*
> *Descends beneath the shadow of the cliffs,*
> *A torrent down the crags. Measured by miles*
> *It is not far from here that the mere lieth;*
> *Rime-frosted groves hang over it, a wood*
> *Fast rooted overshadoweth the wave…*
> *'Tis not a pleasant spot;*
> *Dark towards the clouds the turmoil of the waves*
> *Leaps upward from it, when the tempest stirs*
> *Disastrous storms, until the heaven grows dark*
> *And the skies weep.*[2]

This extract is full of words suggesting danger: "wolf-haunted valleys," "perilous fen paths," "the turmoil of the waves," "disastrous storms," "until the heaven grows dark." Is it too much of an exaggeration to read into these words a description of the fear many felt, and some perhaps still feel, when alone in lonely, deserted places?

There are parts of *Beowulf* that suggest that there is a strong link to Bible imagery, especially the Book of Genesis:

> *The everlasting Lord avenged*
> *The death by which he slew his brother Abel;*
> *Nor gained he by that deed, since for the crime*
> *Far from mankind the Ruler banished him.*
> *Of him all monstrous things were brought to life,*
> *Ogres and goblins and accursed creatures,*
> *And giants, also, who long strove with God.*[2]

J.R.R. Tolkien set *The Hobbit* and the three volumes of *The Lord of the Rings* in an imaginary world, Middle Earth, at the end of the

Third Age. Many attempts have been made to discover whether this can be placed into a European chronology, although this is a fruitless task. Some people have detected elements of Norse, Teutonic and Celtic myths, although the author claimed that it was a new mythology, in an invented world. At times there are echoes of some of the events and landscapes found in *Beowulf* which is, perhaps, unsurprising in view of the fact that the eighth century poem was based on legend and is not firmly rooted in a known landscape.

Tolkien's books are notable for their detailed landscape descriptions and one of the triumphs of the recent films of the books is that the location chosen was New Zealand, a country where so many different landscapes are found in such a small area. However, the films apart, it is an interesting geographical exercise to locate, within Europe, the locations mentioned in the adventures of Frodo, the hobbit, Gandalf, the wizard, and Aragorn, the ranger and eventually, King.

Frodo, Gandalf, Aragorn and the other members of the Fellowship of the Ring are placed in landscapes that demand their response, especially where the environment dwarfs their endeavours. Their adventures and the challenges they faced were from the forces of nature as much as the designs of Sauron, the Dark Lord. At one point they attempted to cross a mountain range called Caradhras and as they proceeded, a growing sense of alarm overwhelmed the group, as snow began to fall and their progress became more and more difficult:

> *While they halted, the wind died down, and the snow slackened until it almost ceased. They tramped on again. But they had not gone more than a furlong when the storm returned with fresh fury. The wind whistled and the snow became a blinding blizzard. Soon even Boromir found it hard to keep going. The hobbits, bent nearly double, toiled along behind the taller folk, but it was plain that they could not go much further, if the snow continued. Frodo's feet felt like lead. Pippin was dragging behind. Even Gimli, as stout as any dwarf could be, was grumbling as he trudged.*
> *The company halted suddenly, as if they had come to an agreement without any words being spoken. They heard*

> *eerie noises in the darkness around them. It may have been only a trick of the wind in the cracks and gullies of the rocky wall, but the sounds were those of shrill cries, and the howls of laughter. Stones began to fall from the mountainside, whistling over their heads, or crashing on the path beside them. Every now and again they heard a dull rumble, as a boulder rolled down from hidden heights above, "We cannot go further tonight", said Boromir, "let those call it wind who will; there are fell voices on the air; and those stones are aimed at us."*[3]

The location of Caradhras may or may not be the Alps; in the context of the book, it does not matter. However, it is relevant to suggest that this passage does describe the feelings of horror that for centuries were the experience of many and particularly, the perception of mountainous regions held by people who did not live in such areas.

In Christian Europe, up to the seventeenth century, mountainous regions were both awe-inspiring and terrifying, places where the individual felt very small and were seen as places where there lurked an evil presence. It was not until the late eighteenth century that people started to see mountains in a different way. Horace Walpole and Thomas Gray were articulating feelings that were to become central to the Romantic Movement's interest in mountains as places of ruin, chaos and catastrophe, where the individual became as nothing in comparison to the majesty and awe-inspiring grandeur of nature. The Alps were seen as potentially dangerous but they did not react to them in horror; they wanted to test themselves to the limits and saw the mountains as a source of wonder and an uplifting of the spirit.

In Christian European tradition monasteries were often built in the Alps, in almost inaccessible locations, such as Grand Chartreuse on Mount Cenis in the French Alps. Such monasteries were away from all human habitation and all distractions. At the most extreme, hermits would live in caves in even more austere conditions. In this particular tradition high mountains were seen as the gateway to heaven or perhaps the border between the physical and spiritual world.

Marjorie Hope Nicolson (1959)[4] in her book, *Mountain Gloom and Mountain Glory*, argued that before the Romantic period, mountain scenery was seen in terms of ruin, chaos and catastrophe.

Romanticism marked a change of taste and aesthetic attitudes to mountain landscapes; a shift from mountains being seen as disorderly and worth avoiding, to the Romantic quest for inspiration in lonely mountain regions. The importance of her book is that it is a comprehensive review of the changing aesthetic that reached its fullest flowering in the Romantic era.

An equally important book is Simon Shama's (1996) seminal work, *Landscape and Memory*. [5] In this book, the author examines the relationship with the landscape around us, in chapters devoted to "Wood" and "Rock." Simon Shama sees two seventeenth century figures as central to the way in which the Romantics viewed mountainous landscapes. The two figures are the theologian (and early geologist) Thomas Burnet and the painter Salvator Rosa.

Thomas Burnet crossed the Alps in 1671 and was repulsed by the wild and chaotic landscape; and yet, at the same time, he was awed and delighted by the vastness and majesty of the views. He wrote *The Sacred Theory of the Earth*[6] in 1684 and argued that mountains had been created by God for the good of mankind. The wildness of mountain landscapes remained but the fear was overcome. In a way, he saw mountains as symbols of fallen mankind and evidence of God's grace: "the world is a ruin, softened in part by God's grace…a wrecked vestige of a former Eden." Seven years after Burnet's book, John Ray, mentioned later, said that mountains were a sign of the wisdom of God, for example, their role in the hydrological cycle, in converting evaporated seawater into the condensed fresh water of rain. Although Thomas Burnet held many views that are rejected by modern science, the seeds of an idea had been sown and would flower in remarkable ways in the writings of some of the Romantic poets.

Salvator Rosa (1615–1673) was an Italian painter and poet who was born near Naples and was noted for his landscapes of rugged mountains and coasts. In a letter to a fellow poet, he described a journey from Ancona to Rome via Assisi and, "the wild beauty of the scenery, a river falling down a half-mile precipice and throwing its foam up again almost as high."[7]

It has been said of Salvator Rosa that he concentrated on macabre objects and it seems beyond doubt that he anticipated the landscapes of the Romantic era. In fact his work only became popular in the nineteenth century, although John Ruskin, who said that his subjects were infected with the "dragon breath" of evil, denigrated it. Salvator Rosa's view of mountains was similar to that of Horace Walpole, in recognising the horror of such areas and being moved by their awesome beauty. In the same letter referred to above he wrote:

> *The journey was beyond all description curious and picturesque; much more so than is the route from here to Florence. There is a strange mixture of savage wildness and domestic scenery, of plain and precipice, such as the eye delights to wander over.... O God! How often have I sighed to possess, how often since called to mind, those solitary hermitages which I passed on my way! — How often wished that fortune had reserved for me such a destiny!* [8]

Two examples of paintings by Salvator Rosa are "Landscape with a bridge," housed in the Galleria Palatina, Palazzo Pitti, Florence and "Landscape with St John the Baptist pointing out Christ," housed in the Glasgow Art Gallery and Museum.

An eighteenth century English traveller, William Gell, visited many areas in the Lake District and wrote about his journey in his diary, *A Tour in the Lakes 1797*. He visited the Fish Inn at Buttermere and described his feelings on seeing Scale Force:

> We saw the amazing fall of Scale Force in the course of the next day, and it is indeed worthy of notice, falling precipitately from the summit of the hill into a chasm scarce six yards wide enclosed on every side but the outlet, by rocks which in some places start up in perpendicular masses and in others hang over in a manner that joined to the height of one hundred and fifty feet perpendicular render the whole tremendous and unrivalled. It is indeed worthy the pencil of a Rosa, the trees covered with moss, the fern starting up in the angles of the rock, and the dashing of the water are highly finished much in his stile (sic). There are two falls, the lower not more than twelve feet in height, nature has left a kind of staircase by the side of it which seems to have been improved by art in order to give a

full view of the higher fall, which otherwise could not have been obtained.[9]

William Gell included a pencil sketch of Scale Force, with some of the characteristics of similar landscapes by Salvator Rosa; a photograph does not have this effect although the precipitate nature of this glacial hanging valley can be shown.

One of Wordsworth's earliest works is "Descriptive Sketches," written when he was twenty three, being an account of a walking tour in the Alps, in the summer of 1790, with his college friend, Robert Jones, later the Rev. Robert Jones of St John's College, Cambridge, whose home area had been the mountains of Snowdonia. In this poem, Wordsworth speaks of the liberating and uplifting emotions felt in the mountains; however, there are references to a darker and more disturbing feeling in mountainous regions:

> *Mid savage rocks, and seas of snow that shine,*
> *Between interminable tracts of pine,*
> *Within a temple stands an awful shrine,*
> *By an uncertain light revealed, that falls*
> *On the mute image and the troubled walls.*
> *Oh! Give not me that eye of hard disdain*
> *That views, undimmed, Einsiedlen's wretched fane.*
> *While ghastly faces through the gloom appear,*
> *Abortive joy, and hope that works in fear;*
> *While prayer contends with silenced agony,*
> *Surely in other thoughts contempt may die.*
> *(Einsiedlen' is a Catholic shrine visited by those suffering in body and mind.)*[10]

Wordsworth saw the high Alps as evidence of the power of God, when he wrote: "*Among the more awful scenes of the Alps, I had not thought of man, or a single created being; my whole soul was turned to Him who produced the terrible majesty before me.*"[11] Wordsworth was using the word "awful" in a way that may sound strange to modern ears. Today, more often than not, the word is used to describe something unpleasant or horrible; we often say that the weather is awful and by that we mean that the weather is unpleasant. However, the word can be used to describe a feeling of reverential wonder; we look upon a spectacular view and our emotions register a feeling of wonder that anything could be so beautiful, in much the same way that the word awesome is often used today.

The poets of the Romantic era often used the word in almost a religious sense, as a means of expressing a view of nature, which placed man in his place as a small and insignificant being when surrounded by the grandeur of the natural world. However, perhaps the most notable use of the word was by Captain Robert Falcon Scott, in his diary entry for 17th January 1912. On reaching the South Pole on this date, he found that he had been beaten by Roald Amundsen, the Norwegian, by a month; in his intense disappointment he wrote, "Great God! This is an awful place." Was this simply an outpouring of his disappointment, or did it also contain an exclamation of the "awfulness" of this remote and deserted place? Many before and since have felt similar emotions when a place has turned one's thoughts to the greatness of God's creation. Such places cause us to think that we are full of awe as we contemplate the wonders of the natural world.

In Wordsworth's "Descriptive Sketches," he spoke of "an awful shrine" and in a letter, he referred to "the more awful scenes of the Alps"; these were not the words of a man repelled by high mountains, but rather one who saw such landscapes almost in a spiritual way. The references to "savage rocks," "awful shrine," "prayer contends with silenced agony," and "awful scenes" and "terrible majesty," all suggest that Wordsworth saw a connection between a sense of awe and the fearful aspect of wild places, a sense that we are, in such landscapes, overwhelmed by the power and grandeur of nature. Another example of the power and grandeur of nature is found later in "Descriptive Sketches":

> *Hail Freedom! Whether it was mine to stray,*
> *With shrill winds whistling round my lonely way,*
> *On the bleak sides of Cumbria's heath-clad moors,*
> *Or where dank sea-weed lashes Scotland's shores;*
>
> *Tonight, my Friend, within this humble cot*
> *Be scorn and fear and hope alike forgot*
> *In timely sleep; and when, at break of day,*
> *On the tall peaks the glistening sunbeams play,*
> *With a light heart our course we may renew,*

The first whose footsteps print the mountain dew.
1791 and 1792

Is there a special quality to remote and lonely places that speaks to our emotions in a way no town or city can ever replicate? One day in July, a school party was walking from the Langdale Valley, following Mill Gill (Stickle Ghyll) on the path up to Stickle Tarn; the weather was fine and the views very clear. However, on the walk down, the cloud cover increased and the views became increasingly obscured, the temperature became much cooler and soon it was raining hard. As the party rested for a few minutes, one girl, from Poole in Dorset, who had never visited the Lakes before, said to me: "How strange it is that even in bad weather, which is frightening in a way, the hills are so beautiful?"

Was this girl, perhaps without thinking, saying something similar to Wordsworth's view of such landscapes? Was she experiencing a sense of awe in the face of changing weather conditions, which in the space of an hour had turned the valley from a sunny July pastoral scene into a misty bleakness with a threat of worsening weather? Indeed, is it perhaps the case that we should look at these remote areas with a spiritual eye'? It is interesting that many Christians see wilderness areas as central to their being. They speak of a wilderness experience as a defining moment in the development of their faith, a means by which they come closer to Jesus and are given the time, space and inspiration to follow their calling more closely. The wilderness experience may be the result of a major change in the circumstances of their life, that temporarily disturbs their peace of mind and composure, or it may be the result of an unexpected turn of events, beyond their control. However, whatever the stimulus, the result is a sudden change that affects every aspect of life.

In a similar way to the student from Poole, Gerald McGuire, once an officer of the Youth Hostel Association and a member of the North York Moors National Park Commission, spoke of the openness of moorland and the dominance of the sky, as helping communion with God:

> It's almost a religious experience. I talked about the wild landscape and the sky, and there's a sense of God being there, Who made it all. It's spiritual in a very big way.[12]

The Beautiful and the Sublime

This last quotation touches upon a line of thinking that developed before the Romantic era but came to fruition during the latter years of the eighteenth and into the nineteenth century. It is discussed at length in Carl Woodring's (1989) book on *Nature and Art*.[13] It is argued that nature can be seen as the work of a Creator and that nature brings glory to the Creator God. If we understand nature in this way, we are on the way to understanding God. These issues will be examined in a later chapter, especially the Bible's view that man is a fallen creature and that nature bears some of the curse upon man because of disobedience in Eden.

In a series of lectures on poetry from 1832 to 1841, John Keble detected the growth of apostasy in nineteenth century England and saw a direct correlation between the decline of interest in orthodox religion and the love of nature. He wrote:

> May it not be by the special guidance of Providence that a love of country and Nature, and of the poetry which deals with them, should be strong, just at the time when the aids which led our forefathers—Holy Scripture, solemn liturgies, and sacramental occasions—have become otherwise far removed from the habit of our daily life.' [14]

Although there was to be a religious revival in the nineteenth century, set in motion by the Oxford Movement, John Keble's argument has a particular resonance in the early years of the twenty-first century, in what some describe as a post-Christian society.

There is a difficulty in defining a landscape as *beautiful* or *sublime*, a difficulty that perhaps can only be resolved by the individual surveying nature. Thomas Burnet (1684) in *The Sacred Theory of the Earth* wrote of mountains in a way that seems to go beyond any concept of beauty:

> There is something august and stately in the Air of these things, that inspires the mind with great thoughts and passions; we do naturally, upon such occasions, think of God and his greatness: and whatsoever hath but the shadow and appearance of Infinite, as all things have that are too big for our comprehension, they fill and over-bear the mind with

their excess, and cast it into a pleasing stupor and admiration.'[15]

In a similar vein, Thomas Gray spoke of the Alps as having "too much danger to give one time to reflect upon their beauties."

Edmund Burke (1757) defined beauty as a social quality that promotes love; sublimity derives from the need for self-preservation; hence our fascination with thunderstorms, hurricanes, volcanoes and waterfalls. Such a definition concentrates on the extremes of nature, the dramatic events that have the effect of putting man in his place. There is, however, another way of considering the sublime, a way that can be demonstrated from the Old Testament. In 1 Kings 19:11–12, God reveals Himself to the prophet Elijah, not in the strong wind or the earthquake or the fire, but rather in "the still small voice." This is in contrast with the thunder and lightning of God's descent upon Mount Sinai in Exodus 19:16–19. Is it the case that one only of these passages is to be described as sublime, or are they both examples of sublimity where man is dwarfed by greater powers beyond understanding or control.

An example of the sublime in Wordsworth's poetry enables us to look in more detail at the changes that had taken place by the late eighteenth and early nineteenth century. In his sonnet, "It is a beauteous evening, calm and free" Wordsworth considers the quiet and calmness of the human mind:

It is a beauteous evening, calm and free,
The holy time is quiet as a Nun
Breathless with adoration; the broad sun
Is sinking down in its tranquillity;
The gentleness of heaven broods o'er the Sea:
Listen! The mighty Being is awake,
And doth with his eternal motion make
A sound like thunder—everlastingly.
Dear Child! Dear Girl! that walkest with me here,
If thou appear untouched by solemn thought
Thy nature is not therefore less divine:
Thou liest in Abraham's bosom all the year;
And worship'st at the Temple's inner shrine,
God being with thee when we know it not.[16]
1807

There are times when even the most sociable of individuals needs space and time apart from others. There are times when the silence of solitude can bring peace to the most tortured mind, the opportunity to think and to meditate. To many people such times can be restorative both to mind and body. This thinking must have been central to Wordsworth's mind when he penned this sonnet. The quality of the light just before and after sunset can be one of the most rewarding experiences in nature, whether this be in the Lake District or any other rural landscape.

Thoughts on *Mountain Gloom and Mountain Glory*

Marjorie Hope Nicholson's book, *Mountain Gloom and Mountain Glory: The Development of the Aesthetics of the Infinite*, was published in 1959 but is not easily available, except in some university libraries. It is, however, an important book detailing the development of a radical change in the way mountainous landscapes are perceived by travellers and writers. The author looked at the seventeenth century in particular and showed that poets and writers looked back at classical writings of Greek and Roman poets. Another important source of information was the Bible, both the Old and New Testament.

In the context of this chapter, the book is important because it identified the feelings and emotions behind some of the views of mountainous and wild landscapes held for centuries, up to the Romantic era. The aesthetic change that took place in the writings of the Romantics has had a powerful influence on the way we view such landscapes and it is not too great an exaggeration to suggest that it was partly responsible for the creation of the National Trust and the National Parks. It is surely significant that, until the creation of the Norfolk Broads National Park, followed by the New Forest in 2005 and lastly the South Downs in 2009, the other ten National Parks are all areas of the country that can be described as wild, remote and unspoilt.

Marjorie Hope Nicolson identified a sense of the sublime in the Old Testament, for example, Isaiah 52:7 (N.I.V.):

How beautiful on the mountains are the feet of those who bring good news, who proclaim peace, who bring good tidings, who proclaim salvation, who say to Zion, "Your God reigns!

It is different in the New Testament, where the emphasis on mountains is different, where mountains are used to describe the proud and the arrogant being brought low?

In Luke 3:5 (N.I.V.), we find John the Baptist saying:

Every valley shall be filled in, every mountain and hill made low. The crooked roads shall become straight, the rough ways smooth.

Yet, the fact remains that Jesus was closest to God in desert or wilderness landscapes.

Most seventeenth century poets responded to nature's smaller rather than her grander aspects. "They loved her best when she was beautiful rather than sublime."[1] In many cases, poets neither liked nor disliked mountains; they were simply uninterested in them and many had never seen a mountain. Although it cannot be claimed that all seventeenth century writers emphasised *Mountain Gloom*, this was the most common emotion. Mountains were used in an allegorical way, particularly in Christian morality, for example, "Prouder than haughty hills, harder than rocks."[2] Although not referring to mountains, the poet Charles Cotton, in 1681, wrote about Chatsworth House in the Peak District and contrasted, "the ugliness of Nature enhancing the beauty of Art: man has triumphed where Nature failed":

Environ'd round with nature's Shames and Ills
Black Heaths, wild rocks, black Crags, and naked Hills,
And the whole prospect so infirm and rude,
Who is it but must presently conclude?
That this paradise, which seated stands
In midst of Deserts and barren Sands
So bright a diamond would look if set
In a vile socket of Ignoble jet,
And such a face the new-born Nature took
When out of Chaos by the Fiat strook.[3]

How different were the feelings of Wordsworth one hundred and seventeen years later, in "Tintern Abbey":

> *I cannot paint*
> *What then I was. The sounding cataract*
> *Haunted me like a passion: the tall rock,*
> *The mountain, and the deep and gloomy wood,*
> *Their colours and their forms, were to me*
> *An appetite; a feeling and a love,*
> *That had no need of a remoter charm,*
> *By thought supplied, nor any interest*
> *Unborrowed from the eye.* [4]

Such was the change in perception and aesthetics between the seventeenth century and the Romantic era of a hundred years later. Such changes are seen in poetry but also in painting and, to an extent, in music. Beethoven's "Pastoral Symphony" must surely be seen as the musical equivalent of much poetry of the period. In Beethoven's symphony we find the joy of being in the country contrasted with the shepherds' unease as the storm approached.

In developing her argument, Marjorie Hope Nicolson explained that during the Renaissance and Reformation, and passing into the seventeenth century, a controversy developed concerning external nature, and mountains and wild places in particular. Genesis describes a perfect creation that was described by God as "very good"; this view was accepted by John Milton in *Paradise Lost* and was the declared view of John Ruskin in the nineteenth century.

However, an alternative view existed and the question was asked as to when mountains appeared on the earth and why? Andrew Marvell (1621–1678) wrote:

> *'Tis not what once it was, the World;*
> *But a rule Heap, together hurl'd*
> *All negligently overthrown,*
> *Gulfes, Deserts, Precipices, Stone* [5]

John Donne (1573–1631) had earlier described the decay of nature and saw the earth as blighted by "warts and pock holes," "The world's proportion disfigured is." [6]

The theological argument behind the ideas expressed by these two poets is not only complicated but, to modern thinking, it is archaic and irrelevant. It all revolves around the argument as to what happened to the earth and mankind at the time of the fall in Eden. Louis Ginzberg (1913) in *The Legends of the Jews* wrote:

> *The conception that the mountains did not originally belong to the earth's form is prevalent in legend.*[7]

The idea that the mountains were not part of God's initial creation could be used to argue that mountains are blemishes on the earth as a result of human sin. The sin of Cain in killing his brother Abel became part of the legend as to the origin of mountains. Louis Ginzberg continues:

> *The earth, which originally consisted of a level surface, became mountainous as a punishment for receiving Abel's blood…and the earth will not become level again until messianic times.*[8]

Similar confusion surrounds what happened to the earth and mankind when Adam and Eve were expelled from the Garden of Eden. Was the punishment for human disobedience limited to man, or was it extended to nature?

The translation of Genesis 3:17 in the 1610 Douay version of the Bible is: "Cursed is the earth in thy work."

In the 1611 King James Version (Authorised Version) it is translated: "Cursed is the ground for thy sake."

Once again it may seem a small distinction to make but it was important in the seventeenth century. It may even have been partly responsible for the perception of many, that mountainous landscapes were the result of human sin. The reasoning may have been, that if the curse of God passed from man to the earth, then nature was also cursed and may have changed in physical appearance?

Milton, in *Paradise Lost* (Book 9, lines 782–784), comments on the Fall of Adam and Eve in these words:

> *Earth felt the wound, and Nature from her seat,*
> *Sighing through all her works, gave signs of woe*
> That all was lost.

46   *Place, Nature and Spirit*

Thomas Burnet in *The Sacred Theory of the Earth*[9,] already quoted in this chapter, explained that Jewish and Christian thinkers agreed about traditions concerning the primitive earth and he gave an example: "That there was no rain from the beginning of the world until the Deluge, and that there were no mountains before the Flood."

The controversy as to the origin of mountains was largely the result of theological arguments. Some weight must be given to a reference in 2 Peter 2:5, as proof that the world was different before the Flood:

> *And God did not spare the ancient world when he brought the flood on its ungodly people, but protected Noah . . . .*

However this verse is read, it is not possible to prove that the earth was very different physically before the Flood. The only certain truth from this verse is that human nature was no different before or after the Flood.

It is, of course, the case that the surface of the earth is subject to constant change, as a result of erosion and deposition, as well as uplift and tectonic movements. However, it is not suggested that these natural processes of change are the same as the changes described in these theological arguments. It is interesting that the Bible does describe changes more in keeping with geographical understanding; in Psalm 104 there is such an example:

> *Who laid the foundations of the earth,*
> *That it should not be removed for ever.*
> *Thou coveredst it with the deep as with a garment:*
> *At thy rebuke they fled;*
> *At the voice of Thy thunder they hasted away.*
> *They go up by the mountains; they go down by the valleys*
> *Unto the place which Thou hast founded for them.*
> *Thou hast set a bound that they may not pass over;*
> *That they turn not again to cover the earth.*
> *He sendeth the springs into the valleys,*
> *Which run among the hills.*
> *They give drink to every beast of the field:*
> *The wild asses quench their thirst.*
> *By them shall the fowls of the heaven have their*
> *habitation,*

> *Which sing among the branches.*
> *He watereth the hills from His chambers:*
> *The earth is satisfied with the fruit of Thy works.*
> *He causeth the grass to grow for the cattle,*
> *And herb for the service of man:*
> *That He may bring forth food out of the earth;*
> *And wine that maketh glad the heart of man:*
> *And oil to make his face shine,*
> *And bread which strengtheneth man's heart.*
> *Psalm 104:5–15 (A.V.)*

These words are the poetic writing of the Psalms but they are closer to an understanding of the natural world than some of the more fanciful theories of some seventeenth century theologians. Even the eighth century theologian, the Venerable Bede, accepted that changes take place over time; but he also argued that the effects of the Flood did have a dramatic effect on the shape of the earth.

During the Reformation, John Calvin, who spent much of his life among mountains, saw all creation as a blessing from God; in his *Institutes* he wrote:

> *God...has manifested Himself in the formation of every part of the world.... On all His works He has inscribed His glory in characters so clear, so unequivocal, and striking, that the most illiterate and stupid cannot exculpate themselves by the plea of ignorance.... But herein appears the vile ingratitude of men, that while they ought to be proclaiming bounties bestowed upon them, they are only inflated with greater pride....*
> *Notwithstanding the clear representations given by God in the mirror of His works, both of Himself and of His everlasting dominion, such is our stupidity that always inattentive to these obvious testimonies, we derive no advantages from them.*[10]

To Calvin, evil existed not in nature but in man; he believed that the earth was the same as it was at creation, including the mountains and all wild landscapes. To Calvin, nature is changed after the Fall, as far as man is concerned, but remains perfect in every other way. This thought arises from the fact that nature is seen as part of God's perfect creation. The emphasis is placed on man's disobedience and increasing wickedness but even this does not alter the glories of nature. It is an interesting speculation as to how Calvin would react to the abuse and pollution of the natural world that has resulted from human exploitation of the planets resources. Much of the environmental debate and the importance of a *green* view of the world is based on the view that mankind has abused and disfigured a pristine planet.

In the context of how attitudes to mountains changed after the seventeenth century, one thing united both sides of the argument. It is perhaps an idea that, to some, appears out of place in the twenty-first century, but the perception of mountains always had a theological basis; it was taken for granted that there was a religious origin to our view of the beautiful and the sublime. Even when a religious belief did not exist in an individual, there was always an awareness of things greater than the human mind and in that broad sense, it was a spiritual feeling.

It cannot be denied that during the eighteenth century the irregularity of mountain landscapes, which at one time had repelled, began to attract. Those who had always seen the grandeur of such landscapes and recognised the sublime but did not see them as beautiful slowly began to see them in a different light. James Thomson, in "The Seasons" (1730), spoke of nature in these terms and in doing so brought together the sublime and the beautiful:

> *Where can we meet with such variety, such beauty, such magnificence? All that enlarges and transports the soul!*[11]

Marjorie Hope Nicolson saw the change in aesthetics very clearly when she wrote:

> *In the new God and the new Nature, the pre-Romantic poets found the source of the Sublime, which makes the descriptive poetry of the eighteenth century very different in structure, style and emphasis from the poetry of the English Renaissance.*[12]

In other words, "Mountain Gloom" may not have completely disappeared but "Mountain Glory" was beginning to appear, reaching its greatest period with the Romantic poets of the late eighteenth and early nineteenth centuries. Instead of mountains being seen as monstrosities, ruined relics of a changed earth, places of horror and alien to the human spirit, more and more people were seeing them as awe-inspiring, places of wonder and sources of delight and inspiration.

James Thomson is regarded as one of the finest British mountain poets before Wordsworth; just as Wordsworth lived among the hills and mountains of the Lake District, Thomson, a Scot, grew up among the hills of Roxburghshire. In the "Winter" section of "The Seasons," he said that Scots:

> *...ask no more than simple nature gives;*
> *They love their mountains, and enjoy their storms.*[13]

In his "Grand Tour" Thomson visited the Alps and wrote about his feelings in such landscapes:

> *...their shaggy mountains charm*
> *More than Gallic or Italian plains;*
> *And sickening fancy oft, when absent long,*
> *Pines to behold their Alpine Views again—*
> *The hollow-winding stream: the vale, fair-spread*
> *Amid an amphitheatre of hills.*[14]

Marjorie Hope Nicolson charted the changing aesthetic of mountain landscapes, and I acknowledge a debt of gratitude to her inspiring thoughts. There can be little doubt that the changing perception of mountains began in the seventeenth century and is found in the poets of the Romantic era, particularly the poetry of William Wordsworth. During that period there was a transition between a theological view of the world and the beginnings of scientific enquiry. At the end of the sixth day of Creation, Genesis records that God saw His work as "very good." The curse upon mankind and the earth followed the Fall of Adam and Eve. During the Romantic era and afterwards there was a growing realisation that the six days of Creation were symbolic of a very great period of time. It was at this time that poets began to see the world from observation rather than from books and legend. "Mountain Gloom" was slowly replaced by "Mountain Glory."

The English traveller in the nineteenth century viewed mountain landscapes in a very different way to Thomas Burnet. Wordsworth in his *Guide to the Lakes* wrote:

> *A stranger to mountain imagery naturally on his first arrival looks out for sublimity in every object that admits of it.*[15]

As the nineteenth century progressed, it became common for travellers to carry with them *Guides* as well as the poetry of Wordsworth, Byron or Shelley, depending on the area of their tour. Is it perhaps the case that as travel became easier, especially to mountainous or remote areas that the anticipation of the traveller was ready to respond to *external* nature?

In the epilogue to her book, Marjorie Hope Nicolson wrote:

> *The Romantic poets no longer needed to argue and debate philosophical theories of either space or time. They were natural heirs to their great tradition of infinity and eternity. The sense of the vastness of nature that once appalled has become part of their goodly heritage, as has the feeling for an irregularity that need not be either justified or condemned.*[16]

The change from "Mountain Gloom" to "Mountain Glory" is seen so clearly in Wordsworth's poetry. In his poem "View from the Top of Black Comb," he explains how he found "tranquil sublimity," as he moved from wildness to serenity:

> *In depth, in height, in circuit, how serene,*
> *The spectacle how pure! —Of Nature's works*
> *In earth, and air, and earth-embracing sea*
> *A revelation infinite it seems;*
> *Display august of man's inheritance,*
> *Of Britain's calm felicity and power!*
>   *1813*

In so much of his greatest poetry there are no feelings of dread and hopelessness. There are times when nature was awe-inspiring but no feelings of mountain gloom, and, as he grew older there is a spiritual transformation, in his mind, from seeing nature as a threat to an overwhelming feeling of nature as a blessing:

The immeasurable height
O woods decaying, never to be decayed,
The stationary blasts of waterfalls,
And in the narrow rent at every turn
Winds thwarting winds, bewildered and forelorn,
The rocks that muttered close upon our ears,
Black drizzling crags that spake by the way-side
As if a voice were in them, the sick sight
And giddy prospect of the raving stream,
The unfettered clouds and regions of the Heavens.
Tumult and peace, the darkness and the light—
Were all like workings of one mind, the features
Of the same face, blossoms upon one tree;
Characters of the great Apocalypse,
The types and symbols of Eternity,
Of first, and last, and midst, and without end.
The Prelude, Book 6 "Cambridge and the Alps"

The Romantic era in poetry and thought has been a powerful influence on the way we view mountains and natural landscapes. It was, arguably, the underlying influence behind the formation of the National Trust and the creation of the National Parks. Could the founders of these national institutions foresee the popularity of such areas or the number of people who see such areas as a means of escape from the pressures of everyday life at the start of the twenty-first century? We should be thankful for these developments and perhaps give more thought to the changes ushered in by the poets and landscape artists of the late eighteenth and early nineteenth centuries.

Chapter 5
In search of the spiritual

The aim of this chapter is to explore the way in which our view of the environment has resulted in a search for spiritual values in our relationship with the natural world, especially in the poetry of William Wordsworth. The last chapter examined the change in the aesthetics of landscape appreciation, especially during the Romantic era. This was partly the result of spiritual issues influencing our view of landscape and the growth of an awareness that mankind has a stewardship role in the use and exploitation of the environment. There is a broadly Judaeo-Christian approach at the heart of this chapter but many of the issues raised can relate to the beliefs and attitudes of other religions.

It is essential that we try to define what is meant by the *spiritual*, primarily in the context of Wordsworth and other poets of the Romantic era. Some see *spirituality* in terms of conventional religious belief, for example, the Christian faith. In the context of this chapter, the spiritual is a much wider concept. Similarly, to talk about spirituality in Wordsworth's poetry is so much more than the identification of religious belief. This concept can be illustrated by reference to three different poets, William Blake, William Wordsworth and Gerard Manley Hopkins.

In 1803 William Blake wrote his poem "Auguries of Innocence" and set a pattern that was repeated in many of the Romantic poets. He clearly looked to nature as the supreme interpreter of the truth of God:

> *To see a world in a grain of sand,*
> *And a heaven in a wild flower,*
> *Hold infinity in the palm of your hand,*
> *And eternity in an hour.*

The poem ends with a reflection on the way we perceive God:

> *God appears, and God is light,*
> *To those poor souls who dwell in night;*
> *But does a human form display*
> *To those who dwell in realms of day.*

In Wordsworth's "Tintern Abbey" poem, he came closest to defining his view of the spiritual in nature:

> *Therefore am I still*
> *A lover of the meadows and the woods,*
> *And mountains; and of all that we behold*
> *From this green earth; of all the mighty world*
> *Of eye and ear,—both what they half create,*
> *And what perceive; well pleased to recognise*
> *In nature and the language of the sense,*
> *The anchor of my purest thoughts, the nurse,*
> *The guide, the guardian of my heart, and soul*
> *Of all my moral being.*

Here the clearest and most revealing thought is Wordsworth's concept of the "anchor of my purest thoughts."

The poet, Gerard Manley Hopkins, a convert from the Anglican to the Roman Catholic faith, wrote of the meaning of Christian faith to him, as a reflection of the beauty of Creation in his poem "Pied Beauty":

> *Glory be to God for dappled things—*
> *For skies of couple-colour as a brinded cow;*
> *For rose-moles all in stipple upon trout that swim;*
> *Fresh-firecoal chestnut-falls; finches' wings;*
> *Landscape plotted and pieced—fold, fallow, and plough;*
> *And all trades, their gear and tackle and trim.*
>
> *All things counter, original, spare, strange;*
> *Whatever is fickle, freckled (who knows how?)*
> *With swift, slow; sweet, sour; adazzle, dim;*
> *He fathers-forth whose beauty is past change:*
>   *Praise him.*

Surely, in this poem, the poet is praising God for what he sees around him in the beauty of the natural world. Using the terms suggested in

Chapter 2 on *personal* landscapes, Gerard Manley Hopkins is praising God for His infinite variety of colour, shade and texture in the beauty of Creation.

At the heart of much of Wordsworth's poetry there is a spiritual view of landscape, people and place. After this chapter, the following three chapters consider some of Wordsworth's poetry in greater detail. In this chapter we consider the growing importance of *green* issues and, in the broadest sense, the link between environment and spirituality; we will consider the link between the Bible and environmental issues, as well as some points that arose from the Reith lectures of 2000.

However, before looking at Wordsworth and today's growing concern for green issues, we need to explore the spiritual in the minds of other thinkers, some of whom may have been an influence on Wordsworth and other poets of the Romantic era.

In Stephen Gill's book, *Wordsworth and the Victorians*,[1] he pointed out that most Victorians saw Wordsworth's poetry as "a spiritually active, empowering force." He quoted four witnesses to support this view.

The first was William Charles Macready, a famous Victorian actor. He believed that Wordsworth's poetry was a "beneficial agent" in his life, "not just a source of pleasure, a superior pastime, but a transforming power and a force for good." In Book 4 of *The Excursion* we find the view that man has always found in nature, intimations of Divinity, which can speak to us in every circumstance:

> *The Wanderer said: —*
> *"One adequate support*
> *For all the calamities of mortal life*
> *Exists—one only; an assured belief*
> *That the procession of our fate, howe'er*
> *Sad or disturbed, is ordered by a Being*
> *Of infinite benevolence and power;*
> *Whose everlasting purposes embrace*
> *All accidents, converting them to good."*
> ....
> *Then as we issued from that covert nook,*
> *He thus continued, lifting up his eyes*
> *To heaven: —"How beautiful this dome of sky;*

> *And the vast hills, in flucuation fixed*
> *At thy command, how awful! Shall the Soul,*
> *Human and rational, report of thee*
> *Ever less than these?"—Be mute who will, who can,*
> *Yet I will praise thee with impassioned voice:*
> *1814*

These words speak of the spiritual impact of the natural world on the human soul. They are not incompatible with traditional Christian belief but such lines raise a question. To what extent is it possible to worship God in nature, where the one who worships holds no orthodox belief?

The second witness to illustrate that Wordsworth's poetry is a "spiritually active, empowering force" is William Hale White (his pseudonym was Mark Rutherford), who was a civil servant and one time theology student. He paid tribute to Wordsworth and said that the poet had helped him form a more easily understood belief in God: "God was brought from that heaven of the books and dwelt on the downs in the far away distances, and in every cloud-shadow which wandered across the valley."

The third witnesses are the two early geologists, William Whewell and Adam Sedgwick. Both men were convinced that God had created the world with a purpose. Sedgwick was a friend of Wordsworth and his writing may have influenced the poet and may have been a source of information concerning the relation of geology and religious belief. In pre-Darwinian times there was not the conflict between geology and religious belief that developed as a result of the publication of *On the Origin of Species* in 1859.

In the case of William Whewell, it may have been the case that Wordsworth was an influence on his work in geology. In his book *Wordsworth and the Geologists*,[2] John Wyatt found words and phrases which seemed to come from the deepest feelings of the poet; the expression of "emotion recollected in tranquillity," which is Wordsworth's definition of poetry in the 1802 preface to *Lyrical Ballads*; other phrases found in Whewell's writing are "scenes of youth," "haunted me" (perhaps a reference to the "haunted me like a passion" in "Tintern Abbey"), and finally the phrase "my heart has leaped up" from the first of Wordsworth's "Poems referring to the period of early childhood":

My heart leaps up when I behold
A rainbow in the sky:
So was it when my life began;
So is it now I am a man;
So be it when I shall grow old,
Or let me die!
The child is father of the Man;
And I could wish my days to be
Bound each to each by natural piety.

The link between Wordsworth and these two early geologists is interesting, and Dennis Dean (1968) in his Ph.D. dissertation on "Geology and English Literature: Crosscurrents 1770–1830"[3] came to the conclusion that: "During the Romantic period in England, literary trends influenced geological theorising; geological theories, conversely, influenced literature." An example of the overlap between Geology and Literature is found in Wordsworth's "Ode: The Pass of Kirkstone" and his "Descriptive Sketches," the result of Wordsworth's trip to the Alps with the Rev. Robert Jones in 1793. In both of these poems Wordsworth reflects the belief of the time that the earth is only a few thousand years old—four thousand years in the "Ode" and six thousand years in "Sketches," the latter in line with Archbishop Ussher's chronology.

The final witness mentioned by Stephen Gill is the Rev. Frederick William Robertson, a theologian whose views verge on Pantheism and who was influenced by Wordsworth's views of nature. In any study of the spiritual in Wordsworth's poetry, we are faced with views held at the time. Towards the end of his life the Oxford Movement, led by John Keble, John Henry Newman and Edward Pusey, tried to restore traditional Catholic teaching within the Church of England. Many were unsure of where Wordsworth stood on Christian belief. Increasingly he was seen as a Pantheist rather than an Anglican or Roman Catholic. Some even questioned whether Wordsworth believed in a personal God; others suggested he was a Quaker and a Roman Catholic cardinal saw him as a Francis of Assisi figure. It has been suggested that Wordsworth's God is described in his "Tintern Abbey" ode:

And I have felt
A presence that disturbs me with the joy
Of elevated thoughts; a sense sublime

Of something far more deeply interfused,
Whose dwelling is the light of setting suns,

It is possible to see many spiritual influences on Wordsworth and these seem to be relevant to the context of this chapter. It has always been the case that Wordsworth was acutely aware of the influence of the Bible and orthodox belief, even though the nature of his Christian belief is more ambivalent.

In Romans 1:20, the apostle Paul referred to God as the Creator:

The invisible things of Him from the creation of the world are clearly seen, being understood by the things that are made, even His eternal power and Godhead; so that we are without excuse.

In the context of Wordsworth's poetry, this is a clearly stated belief that nature reveals God to man. It is in keeping with much of Wordsworth belief in the power of the natural world.

The Reformation theologian, John Calvin, saw all nature as good and was supreme evidence of the goodness of God:

God...hath manifested himself in the formation of every part of the world.... On all his works he hath inscribed his glory in characters so clear, unequivocal, and striking, that the most illiterate and stupid cannot exculpate themselves by the plea of ignorance. ...But herein appears the vile ingratitude of men; that, while they ought to be proclaiming bounties bestowed upon them, they are only inflated with greater pride.... Notwithstanding the clear representations given by God in the mirror of his works, both of himself and of his everlasting dominion, such is our stupidity that, always inattentive to these obvious testimonies, we derive no advantages from them.
(The Institutes of the Christian Religion Book 1)[4]

It seems that until the middle years of the nineteenth century, both poets and theologians were waiting for the time when the old theology could come face to face with the new science. An example of thinking during pre-Romantic times is that of Henry Moore, the Cambridge Platonist, philosopher and poet. Isaac Newton was his pupil and he had some influence on Samuel Taylor Coleridge. Henry

Moore saw evidence of design and plan in nature and wanted to show that all the created universe argued the power and providence of God.

Thomas Burnet was a seventeenth century theologian who wrote an influential book on the history of the Earth, *Sacred Theory of the Earth*,[5] in 1681. Isaac Newton was an admirer of Burnet's theological approach to geological processes. The importance of this book is seen in that Wordsworth copied out sections of it and Coleridge wanted to turn the *Sacred Theory* into poetry. Burnet wanted to bring science and religion together, especially in the Book of Genesis. In keeping with the thinking of the time he believed that mountains were monstrosities of nature and were the result of man's fall from grace in Eden. He tried to link theology and aesthetics:

> *The face of the Earth before the Deluge was smooth, regular, and uniform, without Mountains, and without a Sea…. This smooth Earth…. Had the beauty of youth and blooming Nature, fresh and beautiful, and not a wrinkle, scar or fracture in all its body; no rocks or mountains…. But even and uniform all over.*

This statement may seem strange to modern thinking but it did mark the gradual transition from a view of mountains as places of horror to a view that can be called the sublime; the horror was being replaced by awe. Marjorie Hope Nicolson saw this changing aesthetic in the thinking of Thomas Burnet:

> *Even while he felt their sublimity, he denied that mountains were beautiful; he could not forgive them but he could not forget them.*

Thomas Burnet was possibly the first writer to see a difference between the emotional effects of the sublime and the beauty of nature. In other words, there is no inconsistency in viewing mountains as awe inspiring and beautiful. All is dependent on the one who views the landscape: "Beauty is in the eye of the beholder."

John Ray (1627–1705) was an eminent botanist and naturalist, who in 1691 expressed a view that was later taken up by poets, writers and scientists at the end of the eighteenth and early decades of the nineteenth centuries:

> *There is no occupation more worthy and delightful than to contemplate the beauteous works of nature and honour the infinite wisdom and goodness of God.*[6]

This thought is, in many ways, a restatement of the words of Psalm 104:24 (A.V.):

> *O Lord, how manifold are thy works! In wisdom hast thou made them all: The earth is full of thy riches.*

John Ray was a believer in *natural theology* that asserted that the wisdom and power of God could be understood by studying His creation, the natural world. His philosophy was expressed in his book *The Wisdom of God Manifested in the Works of the Creation*, published in 1691.

John Ray was still alive when Burnet produced his *Sacred Theory* and was more attracted to mountains than Burnet. He wrote:

> *Mountains are very ornamental to the earth, affording pleasant and delightful prospects, both to them that look downwards from them upon the adjacent countries...and to those that look upwards, and behold them from the plains and low grounds.... What a refreshing and pleasure it is to the eye.*

The spiritual influence upon Wordsworth of John Keble has already been mentioned. John Keble gave a series of lectures on poetry from 1832 to 1841, in which he argued that an interest in nature increased as religious observance decreased:

> *May it not be by the special guidance of Providence that a love of country and Nature, and of the poetry which deals with them, should be strong, just at the time when the aids which led our forefathers—holy scripture, solemn liturgies, and sacramental occasions—have become otherwise far removed from the habit of our daily life.*

All of the thinkers and writers that influenced Wordsworth and others during the Romantic era were part of the changing aesthetic in our view of the natural world. They may not have been direct influences but their thinking, their beliefs and their way of looking at the natural world, all find resonance in the changes that took place in the aesthetics of landscape during the Romantic era.

In his book *Environmental Aesthetics* (1996), J. Douglas Porteous[7] put forward the view that spirituality is to be seen as part of a greater wholeness and suggested that our sense of place is conditioned by four relationships that he defined as "attachment, ethics, aesthetics and spirituality." In the context of this chapter we can appreciate the aesthetics of a landscape that we find delightful to the senses; in similar fashion, we can experience the same landscape as a sacred place and view it with reverence and awe, as it touches the spiritual side of our being. If aesthetics can be described as knowledge derived from the senses, then spirituality is understanding by the soul. To many people, the two are seen as virtually the same, indeed some people see aesthetics as a branch of theology.

Wordsworth came close to this understanding in "The Tables Turned," the second of his "Poems of Sentiment and Reflection":

Books! 'tis a dull and endless strife:
Come, hear the woodland linnet,
How sweet his music! On my life,
There's more of wisdom in it.

And Hark! How blithe the throstle sings,
Let Nature be your teacher.

She has a world of ready wealth,
Our minds and hearts to bless—
Spontaneous wisdom breathed by health,
Truth breathed by cheerfulness.

One impulse from a vernal wood
May teach you more of man,
Of moral evil and of good,
Than all the sages can.

Sweet is the lore which Nature brings;
Our meddling intellect
Mis-shapes the beauteous forms of things: —
We murder to dissect.

Enough of Science and of Art;
Close up those barren leaves;
Come forth, and bring with you a heart
That watches and receives.

These are not isolated sentiments and similar thoughts can be found throughout Wordsworth's poetry; even in the next poem, "Lines written in early Spring," we find the same thoughts expressed, that the love and experience of nature is heaven sent and part of nature's holy plan. Wordsworth saw nature with his senses but understood it with his soul and this fact is central to his poetry and possibly his Christian belief. It scarcely matters that the Romantic poets often saw nature in an idealistic or sanitised form. It was the driving force behind their opposition to urban and technological development. Two examples of the view that our rural landscape was under threat are found in William Blake's "Jerusalem" with its "dark satanic mills" and Wordsworth's worried question, "Is there no nook of English ground secure/ From rash assault?"

A recurring theme that runs through much of Wordsworth's poetry and is at the heart of the search for the spiritual is the nature of his Christian belief. It is interesting that Wordsworth's Duddon Sonnets are prefaced by a thirteen-stanza poem addressed "To the Rev. D. Wordsworth." The poem illustrates the puzzle that is Wordsworth's Christian faith. The conventional belief is present, albeit below the surface, in much of the poem:

The mutual nod,—the grave disguise
Of hearts with gladness brimming o'er;
And some unbidden tears that rise
For names once heard, and heard no more;
Tears brightened by the serenade
For infant in the cradle laid.

Similarly, the three sets of "Ecclesiastical Sonnets" show that Wordsworth was keenly aware of the Christian heritage in which he lived, and yet, in so many of his poems it is nature that is worshipped and God is found in the natural world. There were three sources of Christian influence on Wordsworth. The first was his youngest brother, Christopher, who became the Master of Trinity College, Cambridge; second, was Christopher's son, also Christopher, and nephew to William, who became a Canon of Westminster and later, Bishop of Lincoln; the third figure was the Rev. Robert Walker, a Lake District clergyman who served at the Church of the Holy Trinity at Seathwaite in the Duddon Valley; Wordsworth dedicated sonnet eighteen of the "Duddon" sequence to the church and its pastor.

Natural Science or Natural Theology

In so many ways we have examined the way in which science and theology impacted on Wordsworth. The shift in ideas and our understanding of the natural world that took place during the Romantic era and particularly after the publication of Darwin's *Origin of Species* should never be underestimated. We live in a world where science and religion are so often at conflict and where the two views are seen by many as irreconcilable. It was not as clear-cut in Wordsworth's day. Robert M. Ryan (2005)[8] wrote an article on "Wordsworthian Science" in the 1870s and made the point that during the first half of the nineteenth century, theology was really "natural" theology. Most people saw evidence of the Creator in the natural world and most accepted that there was a Creator. As the century continued and after the discoveries of the early geologists, the concept of an initial Creation started to give way to a belief in a gradual Creation in which evolution was seen as a mechanism.

Wordsworth was seen at the heart of the debate with his "Pantheistic" leanings influencing his Christian belief. Robert M. Ryan quotes from the writing of Richard Acland Armstrong, a Unitarian preacher who said in 1898, almost fifty years after Wordsworth's death:

> *Wordsworth's greatest utterances are so great that in their kind they are absolutely unrivalled in the world's literature; they are wholly unique; they are prophecies in a new Scripture; they are a new evangel for mankind; they are the Bible of a new and larger faith...they constitute, perhaps, the mightiest single intellectual influence of the nineteenth century; the only possible rival being that illuminating and penetrating conception associated with the splendid name of Darwin.*

Another quote from the same source suggests that Wordsworth's thinking was very different from conventional belief:

> *He tolerates no longer the idea of God as a Creator outside Nature, but sees the Divine Energy and love in every throbbing fibre of the universe.*

These seem accurate descriptions of much of the spiritual in Wordsworth's poetry and they illustrate, quite graphically, the difference between orthodox and pantheistic belief. The pantheistic approach sees the work of a Creator in nature and believes that nature brings glory to the Creator. However, the Biblical view is that man is a fallen creature because of sin and that nature bears some of the curse upon man from Eden.

It is hoped that this chapter, so far, has helped in the search for the spiritual in Wordsworth's poetry. There seems little doubt that we can reach different conclusions about Wordsworth's Christian belief, dependent on our definition of spiritual. However, if we define the spiritual in a broader sense as encompassing the awe and wonder that the natural world can produce in the human spirit, then there is no doubt that Wordsworth can be described as a sublime, spiritual poet. Ian H. Thompson (2007) in an article titled "William Wordsworth, Landscape Architect"[9] came to an interesting conclusion concerning Wordsworth's later life:

Later in life, Wordsworth's attitude toward nature became more conventionally Christian: Nature is the handiwork of God. When the invisible hand of Art is following Nature, it is also emulating the work of the Creator. In this way Wordsworth could claim an ultimate transcendental authority for his opinions on the aesthetics of landscape. Secularists cannot share such convictions, but landscape architects often invoke the mystical when they talk about being guided by the 'genius loci' or the ' spirit' of the place.

This section of the chapter ends with the thirtieth of Wordsworth's "Miscellaneous Sonnets," in which he considers the quietness of the human mind as an aspect of the sublime and leads us in a reverie of silence in the stillness of nature, truly a spiritual experience in the widest sense:

It is a beauteous evening, calm and free,
The holy time is as quiet as a Nun
Breathless with adoration; the broad sun
Is sinking down in its tranquillity;
The gentleness of heaven broods o'er the Sea;

Listen! The mighty Being is awake,
And doth with his eternal motion make
A sound like thunder—everlastingly.
Dear Child! Dear Girl! That walkest with me here,
If thou appear untouched by solemn thought,
Thy nature is not therefore less divine;
Thou liest in Abraham's bosom all the year;
And worship'st at the Temple's inner shrine,
God being with thee when we know it not.

Any detailed speculation on the meaning of much of this sonnet detracts from the beauty of the language and the silent meditation that surely follows in the mind of the reader. Some may see evidence of a firm Christian belief, whereas others will see a pantheistic worship of nature. J.Douglas Porteous (1996)[10] used the word *epiphany* to describe a transcendental experience, when the poet, and of course, the reader, is taken out of everyday concerns, prompted by the overwhelming nature of the world about us. Sadly, as the century wore on, the notion of a Divine, moral nature came under attack and many people found that it could not survive the publication of Darwin's *Origin of Species*. The Romantic poets felt an emotional relationship with both landscape and those who lived in it or visited it, to everyone "who has an eye to perceive and a heart to enjoy."

This chapter has, so far, been concerned with a search for the spiritual in the poetry of Wordsworth and has considered some of the influences that may have inspired him and others during the Romantic era. An attempt has been made to explore the nature of Wordsworth's Christian belief and a tentative conclusion has been suggested. The traditional Christian beliefs have been overlaid with a strong pantheistic belief that nature itself can bring us to an understanding of Divine truth. It may be wondered why there has been no mention of, arguably, Wordsworth's greatest "Ode: Intimations of Immortality from Recollections of Early Childhood." This is quite deliberate as it will form an epilogue to this book and hopefully bring together some of the themes considered in the book.

Then and Now: Our Wordsworthian Heritage

Is it possible to trace the influence of Wordsworth and other writers of the Romantic era on present day concerns for the environment, in the very different world of the twenty-first century? Has Wordsworth left us a heritage that we can clearly see in the world around us? It is a legitimate question to ask and perhaps difficult to answer. However, in the context of this chapter with its emphasis on the spiritual in Wordsworth's poetry, there are signs that many of today's concerns are an echo of the Romantic era. It has already been noted that the National Trust, formed in 1895, just forty-five years after Wordsworth's death, can trace part of its origin to Wordsworth's 1835 edition of his *Guide to the Lakes*, where the poet describes the area as "a sort of national property, in which every man has a right and interest who has an eye to perceive and a heart to enjoy."

The first example of a modern view of the environment, and our responsibility for its care for future generations, comes from an unlikely source. The *Economist* journal of December 21, 1996, published a leader article titled "Godliness and Greenness"[11] that looked at the reasons why religious believers and environmentalists are lining up together.

The *Economist* article "Godliness and Greenness" examined the link between religion and environmentalism. It emphasised the concern of so many people that environments are being destroyed and asked whether the moral arguments in favour of a Biblical view of the environment, can be reconciled with the belief structures and views on the environment of other religions. The environment, at whatever scale, is a scientific system, consisting of inputs, processes and outputs; abuse of the environment is seen in terms of pollution, degradation or even total destruction. To a much lesser degree are values and morality mentioned when the environment is discussed. There is plenty of evidence that a change is taking place in the way we view the environment and the responsibility we share for its protection. A growing public awareness of global warming has resulted in a greater degree of personal responsibility, for example, the emphasis on *carbon footprints* and the need to reduce the environmental consequences. It is inevitable that the individual feels helpless and most people understand that only national policies of countries around the world can bring about changes. However, the individual can play a part and the public can bring pressure to bear on governments and decision makers. Is it not possible that religion provides the spiritual basis for care of the environment, and this contribution to the debate needs to stand alongside less spiritual arguments. It is not hard to imagine how Wordsworth would have reacted to environmental concerns. He may well have written letters to the national press and may even have put his thoughts into the form of poetry?

It cannot be doubted that many environmentalists are raising issues of concern in ways that go beyond the scientific; questions of morality are frequently raised and, on occasions, sections of the scientific community are accused of irresponsibility and a reckless disregard for the environment of the future. The media in recent years has been full of green issues of concern:

- The burning of fossil fuels and the effects of global warming.
- The processing of nuclear waste.
- Road building and the encroachment of rural areas.
- Building projects and urban sprawl, often on "green field" sites.
- The agricultural practices which caused the outbreak of "mad cow" disease (BSE) and the consequent risks to human health.
- The debate concerning genetically modified crops.
- The speed with which the 2001 outbreak of Foot and Mouth disease spread around the country.

The *Economist* article addressed the Jewish and Christian argument, arising from the Creation record in Genesis and suggested that the Old Testament can be seen as a very "un-green" document:

> *It says that men and women are made in the image of God, a definition that sets them above the rest of nature. In particular, in the 'dominion covenant' of the book of Genesis, God tells Adam and Eve: "Be fruitful, and multiply, and replenish the earth, and subdue it: and have dominion over the fish of the sea, and over the fowl of the air, and over every living thing that moveth upon the earth. (Genesis 1:28)*

Words like "subdue" and "dominion" and the urgency of "multiply" give some grounds for concern, as wrongly applied they point to over-population, cruelty to animals and other evils.

The article does, however, balance this extreme view with an alternative understanding of the Genesis record concerning human impact on the rest of creation:

> *Many Jewish and Christian scholars now argue that when God gave mankind "dominion" over nature, He was not offering them a licence for ruthless exploitation. The intention was simply that man should be God's "steward" on earth, which includes a responsibility to care for the natural world. Islamic scholars have suggested an almost identical concept; that man should consider himself God's "vice-regent" on earth.*[11]

The article highlights the increased ethical dimension to the environmental debate. We all possess mental characteristics that can best be described in terms of our spiritual, moral, social and cultural development. Is it the case that religion and environmentalism are beginning to occupy the same values position?

The Bible and Environmental Issues

Earlier in this chapter there was a quotation from the seventeenth century botanist and naturalist, John Ray, who saw no conflict between his scientific interests and his religious belief. Apart from his main scientific writings he wrote a book titled *The Wisdom of God Manifested in the Works of the Creation* which was very influential in its time. In the context of the crossing of knowledge boundaries, between religion and environmentalism, John Ray would certainly have agreed that environmental issues can, and perhaps should, be discussed by those interested in the care of the environment and those viewing the environment from a Biblical perspective.

The Bible can be seen to adopt two parallel themes:
- The goal of human history is a new creation and a return to God's original intention before it was frustrated by human sin

and freewill, the concept summarised as the "Fall" and which resulted in mankind being banished from the Garden of Eden.
- Wisdom is seen in the Bible as the creative force of God, personified as God's personal agent in creation—the Word of God—"And God said, 'Let there be light': and there was light."

These issues should perhaps inform the thinking of us all, and although we learn about such issues as children, they should continue to be part of our learning process throughout our life, for the decisions we make now will have consequences for our children and future generations. Wordsworth reflected on this very process in the first of his "Poems referring to the period of childhood":

My heart leaps up when I behold
A rainbow in the sky:
So was it when my life began;
So it is now I am a man;
So be it when I shall grow old,
Or let me die!
The Child is Father of the Man;
And I could wish my days to be
Bound each to each by natural piety.
(1804)[12]

These thoughts are central to the epilogue of this book where Wordsworth's "Ode: Intimations of Immortality from Recollections of Early Childhood" is examined as a conclusion to the book. As so often with Wordsworth's poetry, he saw life in its entirety and understood that feelings and emotions in childhood can powerfully influence the adult's view of the world. The concept that *the child is father of the man* can be applied to many areas of life, but perhaps especially to our view of nature and the natural world. To a child everything is seen as black and white. As we grow older things become more complicated, and as we become aware that life is not so simple, we lose something of the clarity of vision of a young child.

In 1994, Robert Vint, an ecologist and geography teacher, helped form the Religious Education and Environment Programme (REEP), founded on the conviction that concern for nature is essential to religion, and that religious awareness has a vital contribution to make in encouraging a respect for nature. REEP was founded to help students, and surely adults as well, to:

- experience the world around them;
- explore the relevance of traditional religious teachings around the world;
- reflect upon these in order to develop and articulate their own beliefs and values concerning the environment and their place within it;
- then find ways to take practical action based upon their own beliefs and values.

In the context of these aims, it is suggested that many of the world's religions are able to develop a spiritual perspective on the environment. In 1998 REEP published *Faiths for a Future*, a resource book for teaching environmental themes in Religious Education. It looks at the nature of spiritual experience and how we can learn from the world around us; followed by sections on the beliefs and values of Buddhism, Christianity, Hinduism, Islam and Judaism.[13]

In 1974 John Passmore, an eminent Australian philosopher and environmentalist, wrote of man's responsibility for the environment: "Ecological problems have been defined as problems arising as a practical consequence of man's dealing with nature." If environmental problems have been caused or made worse by human activity, then it follows that attempted solutions must arise from human values, which may involve a spiritual dimension. Is this not another way of expressing the "stewardship" role of mankind?[14]

It can be argued that Judaism and Christianity have made it possible to exploit nature in a mood of indifference to the feelings or fate of natural objects. Since both religions have always maintained that it is idolatry to attribute spirit to all other animate and inanimate parts of creation, we are warned to worship the Creator and not the Created. Even so, Francis of Assisi, in the thirteenth century, argued that all creatures have souls and are designed for the glorification of their Creator. His poem "Canticle of Brother Sun" is an expression, albeit unorthodox, of his respect for all Creation, as designed to give glory to God. It may be argued that this approach has no basis in the Bible but it is an approach that shows a reverence towards all of God's creation:

Most High, all-powerful, good Lord,
Yours are the praises, the glory, the honour, and all blessing.
To You alone, Most High, do they belong,
And no man is worthy to mention Your Name.
Praised be You, my Lord, with all Your creatures,
Especially Sir Brother Sun,
Who is the day and through whom You gave us light.
And he is beautiful and radiant with great splendour;
And bears a likeness of You, Most High One.
Praised be You, my Lord, through Sister Moon and the stars,
In heaven You formed them clear and precious and beautiful.
Praised be You, my Lord through Brother Wind,
And through the air, cloudy and serene, and every kind of weather
Through which You give sustenance to Your creatures.
Praised be You, my Lord, through Sister Water,
Which is very useful and humble and precious and chaste.
Praised be You, my Lord, through Brother Fire,
Through whom you light the night
And he is beautiful and playful and robust and strong.
Praised be You, my Lord, through our Sister Mother Earth,
Who sustains and governs us,
And who produces varied fruits with coloured flowers and herbs.
Praised be You, my Lord, through those who give pardon for Your love
And bear infirmity and tribulation.
Blessed are those who endure in peace
For by You, Most High, they shall be crowned.
Praised be You, my Lord, through our Sister Bodily Death,
From whom no living Man can escape.
Woe to those who die in mortal sin.
Blessed are those whom death will find in Your most holy will,
For the second death shall do them no harm.
Praise and bless my Lord and give Him thanks

And serve Him with great humility.[15]

It is however, possible to see the Bible as a source of a human-centred ethic that legitimises the exploitation of nature for human ends; equally, it is possible to praise the Bible for its reverence for nature and the ethic of responsible stewardship of the earth's resources. A contradiction exists, therefore, which is perhaps responsible for the different views on our responsibility towards the environment.

It is instructive to look at some of the themes that run through the Old and New Testaments concerning the environment and our responsibility towards the rest of creation:

OLD TESTAMENT

- Genesis established man's domination over the whole of creation; however, the real question is whether this is a despotic domination, or one where man is expected to exercise responsibility. Are we always sure where we stand?
- There seems to be no Biblical evidence for supposing that man's dominion is in any way despotic; Genesis 2:15 is perfectly clear in its teaching: "The Lord God took the man and put him in the Garden of Eden to work it and take care of it." (N.I.V.)
- The Law of Moses set clear limits to human dealing with nature, for example, there are regulations concerning the treatment of fruit trees, the care of oxen and mother birds, as well as the care of fallow land.
- In Proverbs 12:10 we are told that, "A righteous man cares for the needs of his animal, but the kindest acts of the wicked are cruel."
- The last five chapters of the Book of Job dramatically put the ignorance of mankind in stark contrast to the majestic power of God in His glorious Creation. The Book of Job can be seen as a drama in poetic form, where the wisdom of God is shown in stark contrast to human wisdom. The last five chapters of the Book of Job ask questions, to which no world religion can supply satisfactory answers.

NEW TESTAMENT

- An overriding principle of Christian belief is that we have been freed from the constraints of the Law of Moses, into the liberty that comes from Jesus Christ and His redeeming work; however, the Old Testament is still Scripture and must not be dismissed as being of no importance to the Christian.
- We have to develop a clear view of how Jesus Christ saw and valued the natural world. Two verses in the Gospels speak volumes:
  - Matthew 10:29, "Are not two sparrows sold for a penny? Yet not one of them will fall to the ground apart from the will of your Father."
  - Luke 12:6, "Are not five sparrows sold for two pennies? Yet not one of them is forgotten by God."
- Jesus regarded nature, not only as a resource, but also as an asylum and a source of renewal. Luke 12:27, "Consider how the lilies grow. They do not labour or spin. Yet I tell you, not even Solomon in all his splendour was dressed like one of these." There is no doubt that Jesus enjoyed natural beauty and should not believers follow His example and give glory to God for the wonders of His creation.
- In the Parable of the Lost Sheep, we are being taught a lesson; in the context of the ninety-nine sheep, one lost is not really significant; in fact, the effort to find the lost one was, in economic terms, of marginal value and yet, no effort is spared to find the lost sheep.
- Similarly, in John 10:11, the fact that Jesus lays down His life for His sheep surely says something to us of God's concern for His creation.

Critics of this view will argue that other New Testament passages show that Jesus held a despotic view of other parts of creation. The only passages critics quote are: Matthew 8:28–34, Mark 5:1–17, Luke 8:26–37 (the Gadarene swine) and Mark 11:12–20 (the fig tree cursed); in both cases, a surface view of the incidents, must be seen in the context of a deeper spiritual meaning.

In the light of these examples it can, surely, be demonstrated that the whole tenor of the Old and New Testaments precludes a despotic and anthropocentric attitude. All through Christian history there has been, in the main, a more responsible view of man's dominion over nature. This is not to say that abuses of the environment do not exist, only that the Bible does not give sanction to such abuses.

A conflict has always existed between the philosophy of those religions that are oriented towards nature, as a place of divine revelation, a place where humanity has by ritual and behaviour to attune itself, and the Biblical tradition that has seen history and human society as the arena of primary concern. This has resulted in a view that regards society as separate and subordinate to human history. Many of the world's religions argue that Judaeo-Christian religious experience may not have a proper view of the environment.

The Bible is about human experience and is to that extent, human centred. Yet the fact remains that nature and society are interdependent. All human history is set in actual environments and this has shaped the attitudes of the Biblical writers, who wrote in a predominantly rural society in the Mediterranean highlands that subsisted on a mixed agricultural economy, including the cultivation of grass and fruits and the herding of sheep and goats.

The Bible teaches that human life began from the dust of the earth and returns to dust after death. All the events in the Bible are to be seen in the context of a rural society, dependent on the bounties of nature and much Biblical prophecy saw natural degradation and disaster as the punishment for sin. Much of the ritual of Hebrew religion, as well as the Law of Moses, concerns the natural cycle of the agricultural year; features of the landscape, springs, trees, mountains, thunderstorms, all feature in the Biblical record of man's contact with God.

Although much of the preaching of Jesus Christ can only be fully understood in the context of a rural society, it is only in the New Testament that humanity becomes increasingly urban and the centre of Christianity becomes the city. Finally, it is in the New Testament that we find the idea of stewardship on behalf of God. John Calvin in the sixteenth century resuscitated this idea, applying it to our possession and care of the earth as a whole; he decried the "plundering of the earth of what God has given it for the nourishment of man" as frustrating God's goodness.[16]

Similarly, Sir Matthew Hale, an English judge and amateur theologian, wrote in 1677,

> *The end of man's creation was that he should be God's viceroy...steward. Man was endowed with this dominion, trust and care...to preserve the face of the earth in beauty, usefulness and fruitfulness.*[17]

Here, surely, is a view of the environment that many would subscribe to in the early days of the twenty-first century.

There are many indications that the world is becoming increasingly environmentally conscious. Even if a cynic may argue that statements from governments and international organisations can be more in the form of politically correct statements, not always leading to action, it cannot be denied that global environments and life-supporting systems are the concern of scientists, the public and environmental organisations. The difference between the economically more developed countries and the economically less developed countries is not only recognised, but is seen as one of the most serious constraints on global action. However, all sectors of the global community were represented at such conferences as the "Rio Earth Summit" in 1992, which set up "Agenda 21," the Kyoto Agreement in 1997, and the 2000 Hague Conference. Since then there has been an increased political debate on the local, national and international scale.

BBC Reith Lectures 2000

The six lectures in the Reith cycle 2000 covered a wide range of global environmental issues, under the heading of sustainable development, which two of the five lecturers described as "enlightened self-interest." The series concluded with the views of the Prince of Wales and a discussion involving all the Reith lecturers. In his personal statement, the Prince of Wales injected a note of caution.

> *I am convinced we all need to dig deeper to find the inspiration, sense of urgency and moral purpose required*

> *to confront the hard choices which face us on the long road to sustainable development.*[18]

Many of the arguments put forward by the Prince of Wales were a restatement of opinions he had expressed over many years; however, in the context of the Reith Lectures 2000 theme, they carried considerable force, even though some of his views are not acceptable to many in the scientific community. In the context of this chapter, Prince Charles was aligning himself with the view that religion may provide the spiritual basis for care of the environment. Several lengthy extracts from his lecture illustrate the extent of his argument:

> *The idea that there is a sacred trust between mankind and our Creator, under which we accept a duty of stewardship for the earth, has been an important feature of most religious and spiritual thought throughout the ages. Even those whose beliefs have not included the existence of a Creator have, nevertheless, adopted a similar position on moral and ethical grounds. It is only recently that this guiding principle has become smothered by almost impenetrable layers of scientific rationalism. I believe that if we are to achieve genuinely sustainable development we will have to rediscover, or re-acknowledge, a sense of the sacred in our dealings with the natural world, and with each other. If literally nothing is held sacred anymore—because it is considered synonymous with superstition or in some other way "irrational"—what is there to prevent us treating our entire world as some "great laboratory of life" with potentially disastrous long term consequences.*[19]

Is it too much of a flight of the imagination to surmise that Wordsworth would have agreed with such words and, if he were alive today, would have been one of the Reith lecturers?

In a section of his lecture, the Prince of Wales discussed the rapid advances in scientific understanding, particularly in genetically modified crops, and recognised that this is a source of much debate and argument. He referred to the writings of Rachel Carson, particularly "Silent Spring," published in 1962.[20] She was one of the main voices, at the time, which questioned the use of modern synthetic pesticides and their effect on food chains. It was this book, more than anything else at the time, which contributed to the increasing ecological and conservationist attitudes that emerged in the 1960s and 1970s, attitudes that have become of urgent concern in the 1990s and into the present century. Rachel Carson reminded us that we do not know how to make a single blade of grass, and the Prince of Wales went on to remind us of New Testament values:

> *St. Matthew emphasised that not even Solomon in all his glory was arrayed as the lilies of the field (the words of Jesus in the Sermon on the Mount—Matthew 6:28–30). Faced with such unknowns it is hard not to feel a sense of humility, wonder and awe about our place in the natural order. And to feel this at all stems from the inner heartfelt reason, which sometimes, despite ourselves, is telling us that we are intimately bound up in the mysteries....do you not feel that, buried deep within each and every one of us, there is an instinctive, heart-felt awareness that provides—if we will allow it to—the most reliable guide as to whether our actions are really in the long term interests of our planet and all the life it supports? This awareness, this wisdom of the heart, maybe no more than a faint memory of a distant harmony, rustling like a breeze through the leaves, yet sufficient to remind us that the earth is unique and that we have a duty to care for it. Wisdom, empathy and compassion have no place in the empirical world, yet traditional wisdom asks, "Without them are we truly human?" and it would be a good question. It was Socrates who, when asked for his definition of wisdom, gave as his conclusion, "knowing that you do not know."*[21]

Many will question, or even deny, the force of these arguments; others may accept some of the Prince's points but see other issues as unscientific, or an attempt to put restrictions on scientific enquiry. There will be others who accept and endorse the whole thrust of the argument and see the lecture as a welcome reminder of the spiritual nature of our being and the responsibility we have towards the stewardship of the planet.

And He said also unto His disciples, "There was a certain rich man, which had a steward; and the same was accused unto him that he had wasted his goods. And he called him, and said unto him, How is it that I hear this of thee? Give an account of thy stewardship; for thou mayest be no longer steward."
Luke 16:1–2 (A.V.)

There are two sides to every coin—two ways of looking at each generation's responsibility for the environment. The conclusion however is the same. We can either take the view that our children inherit the world we bequeath to them; or take notice of the values of the North American Indians: "We do not inherit the earth from our parents; we borrow it from our children."

Chapter 6
Wordsworth and the Bliss of Solitude

At the heart of this book is the belief that nature can be viewed with spiritual eyes and that place and landscape can speak to the deepest realms of the human spirit. In Christian terms it is the belief that the wisdom of God is revealed in the whole of Creation, a view that is shared by many other religions. Apart from religious belief, it is contended that the spirit of a place can illuminate and enrich the human spirit. There are many different ways in which the Romantic era changed our thinking and the period from 1770–1850 was a period of greatest change in the aesthetics of place and landscape.

The poetry of William Wordsworth illustrates these sentiments and his inspiration came largely from a deep understanding of place, particularly, but not exclusively, the landscape of the English Lake District. An example of Wordsworth's ability to view a landscape with the eyes of a geographer and yet, at the same time, see the landscape with spiritual eyes is the poem he wrote about a mapmaker on Black Combe, south west of Duddon Bridge (G.R. 136855). The poem is titled "Written with a slate pencil on a stone, on the side of the mountain of Black Comb(e)" and is dated 1813:

> *Know, if thou grudge not to prolong thy rest,*
> *That on this summit whither thou art bound,*
> *A Geographic Labourer pitched his tent,*
> *With books supplied and instruments of art,*
> *To measure height and distance: lonely task,*
> *Week after week pursued! —To him was given*
> *Full many a glimpse (But sparingly bestowed*
> *On timid man) of Nature's processes*
> *Upon the exalted hills...*

> *The whole surface of the outspread map,*
> *Became invisible: for all around*
> *Had darkness fallen—unthreatened, unproclaimed—*
> *As if the golden day itself had been*
> *Extinguished in a moment: total gloom,*
> *In which he sate alone, with unclosed eyes,*
> *Upon the blinded mountain's silent top.*

Leaving aside the dubious choice of a campsite, John Bate (1991) made a telling point concerning the linking together of different areas of knowledge:

> There is a strong analogy between poet and geographer, poem and map; the poet writes his text on a stone on the side of a mountain, while the mapmaker turns the mountain into a text. The poem ends with sudden darkness as the mist comes down; geographer and poet are reminded that nature cannot always be seen, controlled, and mapped—it must be respected.[1]

In this poem the mapmaker appears to be in control, the master of his attempt to accurately display the mountain in the form of a map. He has the skill and the tools needed for the task, but there is a sense in which "nature's processes upon the exalted hills" will always dwarf a sense in which nature is in control and the efforts of "timid man" are put firmly in place. We are allowed a glimpse of nature but it is "sparingly bestowed."

Nature's processes are revealed to the poet and are recorded; the landscape is recorded on the map by the "geographic labourer." Are we not being told that the landscape can be revealed through the poem and through the map to anyone who may not have visited it, or perhaps recollected by someone who has visited the scene? The medium can be either the poem or the map. If this is the case then landscape can certainly be experienced in a map, but perhaps, more importantly, in poetry that can inform the mind and comfort the soul when away from the scene. Wordsworth could bring to his mind the "wild secluded scene" of the River Wye, even in hours of weariness and "mid the din of towns and cities":

> *These beauteous forms,*

> *Through a long absence have not been to me*
> *As is a landscape to a blind man's eye;*[2]

Is this possibly a reason for saying that the study of place and landscape can almost be, in the widest sense, a spiritual experience? Should a study of landscape instil a sense of wonder in the observer? Bate (1991) argued that Romantic poetry, particularly that of Wordsworth "derives from place; it repays its debt to geography by spiritualising the sides which are its source."[3] In similar vein, Laurence Goldstein (1977) wrote of Wordsworth's sense of place and the feelings that emanate from valued places:

> Wordsworth's poetry made something happen; it awakened the moral conscience of posterity to the value of places which bear an habitual resemblance to Eden, our profound dream of harmony and joy. And our own joy owes much of its body to Wordsworth's recollections and his feelings in those places. Magical presences haunt the sites of Hawkshead, or Esthwaite Water, or the daffodils of Gowbarrow Park because Wordsworth felt and articulated their character.[4]

When at school in Hawkshead, one of Wordsworth's favourite walks in the evening was along the shore of Esthwaite Water; there was a seat, built by the Reverend William Braithwaite, under a yew tree. Wordsworth included a poem in the 1798 edition of "Lyrical Ballads": "Lines left upon a seat in a Yew-tree which Stands near the Lake of Esthwaite, on a Desolate part of the Shore, yet Commanding a Beautiful prospect."

> *Nay, Traveller! Rest. This lonely yew-tree stands*
> *Far from all human dwelling; what if here*
> *No sparkling rivulet spread the verdant herb;*
> *What if the bee love not these barren boughs?*
> *Yet, if the wind breathe soft, the curling waves,*
> *That break against the shore, shall lull thy mind*
> *By one soft impulse saved from vacancy*
>
> *1795*

The poem was started while Wordsworth was still at school and shows that, at an early age, he was able to describe the spirit of a place, moving from expressions of sentiment concerning the character of the one who built the seat and, finally, addressing the way in which we can mould our character and learn from the experience of others. In this poem the death of the one who built the seat leads Wordsworth to think of the purity of young imagination, with a word of warning to those whose eyes never contemplate the glories of nature:

> *If thou be one whose heart the holy forms*
> *Of young imagination have kept pure,*
> *Stranger! henceforth be warned; and know that pride,*
> *Howe'er disguised in its own majesty,*
> *Is littleness; that he who feels contempt*
> *For any living thing, hath faculties*
> *Which he has never used; that thought with him*
> *Is in its infancy. The man whose eye*
> *Is ever on itself doth look on one,*
> *The least of Nature's works, one who might move*
> *The wise man to that scorn which wisdom holds*
> *Unlawful ever.*

This early poem shows clearly the view of nature which was to characterise so much of Wordsworth's later poetry, the idea that we are a very small part of the grandeur of nature and that we can only begin to know ourselves by the way we view the natural world, ideally in silent contemplation, as suggested in the last lines of the poem:

> *True dignity abides with him alone*
> *Who, in the silent hour of inward thought*
> *Can still suspect, and still revere himself,*
> *In lowliness of heart.*

In this poem we see how Wordsworth used places to experience various emotions and to set his imagination to work; places affect his thinking and that can lead to thoughts that can best be described as spiritual in their impact on himself and the mind of the reader. Wordsworth was expressing a feeling that is so easily lost, in the twenty-first century, for the busy lives we all lead leave us with little time to reflect on places and emotions. The Welsh poet, William Henry Davies expressed the experience of so many in a poem of

1916, titled "Leisure." He identified feelings that should inspire us to look to nature as a source of solace and spiritual renewal:

What is this life if, full of care,
We have no time to stand and stare?

No time to stand beneath the boughs,
And stare as long as sheep and cows:

No time to see, when woods we pass,
Where squirrels hide their nuts in grass:

No time to see, in broad daylight,
Streams full of stars, like skies at night:

No time to turn at Beauty's glance,
And watch her feet, how they can dance:

No time to wait till her mouth can
Enrich that smile her eyes began?

A poor life this if, full of care,
We have no time to stand and stare.

The best known of Wordsworth's "Poems of the Imagination" is number twelve, better known as "Daffodils::

I wandered lonely as a cloud
That floats on high o'er vales and hills
When all at once I saw a crowd,
A host of golden daffodils;
Beside the lake, beneath the trees,
Fluttering and dancing in the breeze.

Continuous as the stars that shine
And twinkle on the milky way,
They stretched in never-ending line
Along the margin of a bay:
Ten thousand saw I at a glance
Tossing their heads in sprightly dance.

The waves besides them danced, but they
Out-did the sparkling waves in glee:
A poet could not but be gay,
In such a jocund company;

*I gazed—and gazed—but little thought
What wealth the show to me had brought;*

*For oft, when on my couch I lie
In vacant or in pensive mood,
They flash upon that inward eye
Which is the bliss of solitude;
And then my heart with pleasure fills,
And dances with the daffodils.*

The ideas developed beside Esthwaite Water during "the silent hour of inward thought" are again revealed in this best known of all Wordsworth's poems. His "inward eye" illuminated his soul and his view of nature brought to him the rarest of emotions, which he simply described as the "bliss of solitude." The process of the poet's thinking is clear in this poem, for what starts off as a description of a lake-side scene, moves into reverie as the poet muses on the beauty of the location, and finally shows us how remembering the scene amongst the distractions of life can bring comfort to the soul. A spiritual feeling arises from a landscape description and this is typical of much of Wordsworth's poetry of place.

The background to "Daffodils" was a walk Wordsworth enjoyed with his sister, Dorothy on April 15th 1802, from the home of their friend, Thomas Clarkson in Eusemere at the northern end of Ullswater. They had walked along the shore of the lake towards Aira Force, Gowbarrow Park and Patterdale. The location of the walk was obviously important, and the sight of the daffodils by the shore made a deep impression on Wordsworth and his sister. Dorothy described the walk in her journal for that day:

It was a threatening, misty morning, but mild.... The wind was furious...and seized our breath. The lake was rough.... The hawthorns are black and green, the birches here and there greenish, but there is yet more of purple to be seen on the twigs. We got over into a field to avoid some cows—people working. A few primroses by the roadside—woodsorrel flower, the anemone, scentless violets, strawberries, and that starry, yellow flower which Mrs. C. calls pile wort. When we were in the woods beyond Gowbarrow Park we saw a few daffodils close by the water-side. We fancied that the lake had floated the seeds ashore, and that the little colony had so sprung up. But as we went along there were more and yet more; and at last, under the boughs of the trees, we saw that there was a long belt of them along the shore, about the breadth of a country turnpike road. I never saw daffodils so beautiful, they grew among the mossy stones about them; some rested their heads upon these stones as on a pillow for weariness; and the rest tossed and reeled and danced, as if they verily laughed with the wind, that blew upon them over the lake; they looked so gay, ever glancing, ever changing. The wind blew directly over the lake to them, there was here and there a little knot, and a few stragglers a few yards higher up; but there were so few as not to disturb the simplicity, unity, and life of that one busy highway. We rested again and again.[5]

The scene Dorothy described can still be appreciated today, even though the traffic on the main road to Patterdale and the Kirkstone Pass can destroy some of the quietness of the location. It may make the lakeside woods and the daffodils difficult to view in peace and solitude. Even so, to sit in the woods by the shores of Ullswater, in spring, surrounded by daffodils and the view across the lake, it is still possible to experience upon "the inward eye" the same "bliss of solitude."

It is obvious that Dorothy, as well as William, was enchanted by the prospect on that April day in 1802. Some of Dorothy's journal entries use the same words as are found in the poem: "they tossed and reeled and danced…they looked so gay"; it is almost as if we hear the brother and sister talking in the phrases of the poem. It is possible that we see in the poem and the journal, evidence of the joy that they both experienced, when they walked together in the open air, near lakes and in the mountains. Two weeks after the walk along the shore of Ullswater, Dorothy recorded in her journal, a walk to John's Grove, named after their brother, John, and she described the scene among the trees beside Grasmere Lake:

We then went to John's grove, sate a while at first. Afterwards William lay, and I lay, in the trench under the fence—he with his eyes shut and listening to the

> *waterfalls and the birds. There was no one waterfall above another—it was a sound of waters in the air—the voice of the air. William heard me breathing and rustling now and then, but we both lay still, and unseen by one another; he thought that it would be as sweet thus to lay so in the grave, to hear the peaceful sounds of the earth, and just to know that our friends are near. The lake was still; there was a boat out. Silver How reflected with delicate purple and yellowish hues...*[6]

It is still possible to walk the same path through the woods, surrounded in spring by carpets of bluebells, to listen to the "sound of waters in the air" and to feel the closeness of friends and see beyond the everyday cares and concerns. It is to experience the spirit of a place, speaking to those sensitive enough to hear its voice and with the wisdom to allow a response in the imagination.

A Digression

Wordsworth's feeling of the spirit of a place is present in much of his greatest poetry and is perhaps the single most important characteristic of his work, the essence of his genius. In order to see this quality at its most sublime, it is necessary to leave the Lake District and travel south to the Wye Valley. If Romanticism can be defined in terms of the intense experience of feelings and imagination, then Wordsworth's "Lines written a few miles above Tintern Abbey" must be a defining experience. On revisiting the banks of the Wye during a tour, July 13th 1798 we have thoughts and emotions that are alone sufficient to place Wordsworth in a place of honour in the Romantic era.

"Tintern Abbey" is a poem in which Wordsworth meditates on the rural scene and the feelings engendered by a much-loved landscape, seen after an absence of five years. It is a poem in which we learn much about the character of the poet and those things that pleased and inspired him. In one respect, above all others, there is a similarity between "Daffodils" and "Tintern Abbey," as similar emotions are stirred by the landscape; the places described have undoubted attractive qualities but, in many ways, those qualities are compared to other places where very different emotions are aroused. Wordsworth wrote in a style and with the same intensity of feeling as did Beethoven in the first movement of his "Pastoral" symphony, in which bird song is the main theme, only to be contrasted later by a violent storm. Beethoven titled the first movement of the symphony, "Awakening of happy feelings on arriving in the country." These same feelings flooded into Wordsworth's mind on revisiting the Wye and he described the circumstances in which the poem was written and the feelings he felt at the time:

> No poem of mine was composed under circumstances more pleasant for me to remember than this: I began it upon leaving Tintern, after crossing the Wye, and concluded it just as I was entering Bristol in the evening, after a ramble of four or five days, with my sister. Not a line of it was altered, and not any part of it written down till I reached Bristol.[7]

It was, therefore, the result of several days musing and absorbing the landscape, which brought to mind less pleasant locations and more troubled thoughts. Here we have an understanding, that in times of turmoil and amidst the stresses of everyday life, it is still possible to obtain solace and refreshment, by thinking of places and circumstances of peace and calm and in many ways this is a spiritual insight. It can be the same when sleep is difficult and many thoughts and concerns keep flooding into our mind. At such times it can be a help to remember places and memories that are pleasant to remember.

As with Dorothy's description of their walk to John's Grove, the sound of the river Wye is as important as the scenes to the eye: "the sweet inland murmer" refers to the fact that the Wye, a few miles above Tintern, is not affected by tides. Wordsworth later wrote of the river: "The Wye is a stately and majestic river from its width and depth, but never slow and sluggish; you can always hear its murmer. It travels through a woody country, now varied with cottages and green meadows, and now with huge and fantastic rocks."[8] The emotions stirred by this return to the River Wye may have been the inspiration over twenty later when Wordsworth devoted thirty-four sonnets to the "Lordly" and "Majestic" River Duddon in southwest Cumbria, the subject of Chapter 8 of this book.

88 Place, Nature and Spirit

The first twenty-two lines of "Tintern Abbey" not only set the scene but they expose the feelings of the poet. All the word pictures in this section of the poem describe peaceful, quiet and comforting scenes. Wordsworth preferred to experience the countryside alone, or perhaps with his sister. Even the reference to "vagrant dwellers" and the lone hermit has the effect of describing people at peace with themselves and their environment:

> *Five years have passed; five summers, with the length*
> *Of five long winters! And again I hear*
> *These waters, rolling from their mountain springs*
> *With a soft inland murmer.—Once again*
> *Do I behold these steep and lofty cliffs,*
> *That on a wild secluded scene impress*
> *Thoughts of more deep seclusion; and connect*
> *The landscape with the quiet of the sky.*
> *The day is come when I again repose*
> *Here, under this dark sycamore, and view*
> *These plots of cottage-ground, these orchard tufts,*
> *Which at this season, with their unripe fruits,*
> *Are clad in one green hue, and lose themselves*
> *'Mid groves and copses. Once again I see*
> *These hedgerows, hardly hedgerows, little lines*
> *Of sportive wood run wild; these pastoral farms*
> *Green to the very door; and wreathes of smoke*
> *Sent up, in silence, from among the trees,*
> *With some uncertain notice, as might seem,*
> *Of vagrant dwellers in the houseless woods,*
> *Or of some hermit's cave, where by his fire*
> *The hermit sits alone.*
>
> (Lines 1–22)

At times in his poetry, as in the lines above, Wordsworth was influenced by the "Picturesque" style; in lines seven and eight, the thought of the landscape connected to the sky is a reference to William Gilpin's "Observations on the River Wye" (1782) where Gilpin first mentions this point:

> Many of the furnaces on the banks of the river consume
> charcoal which is manufactured on the spot, and the

smoke (which is frequently seen issuing from the sides of the hills, and spreading its thin veil over a part of them) beautifully breaks their lines, and unites them with the sky.[9]

It is significant that Wordsworth does not mention the industrialisation of some parts of the countryside. Jonathan Bate (1992)[10] makes the point that Wordsworth mentions smoke from cottages but not the coal barges from Ironbridge and the industrial smoke in the Wye Valley, which are mentioned by Gilpin. In this respect Wordsworth was describing an idealised landscape, held forever in his mind, where nothing intrudes to spoil what he saw as perfect.

The next section of the poem expresses the poet's love of this "wild secluded scene" and the thoughts of more deep seclusion that comforts his soul when away from this landscape:

These beauteous forms,
Through a long absence have not been to me
As is a landscape to a blind man's eye;
But oft, in lonely rooms, and mid the din
Of towns and cities, I have owed to them,
In hours of weariness, sensations sweet,
Felt in the blood, and felt along the heart,
And passing even into my purer mind
With tranquil restoration;

(Lines 23–31)

There are in these lines references to the spiritual side of Wordsworth's character, his "purer mind" that was restored by thoughts of the Wye Valley. His "tranquil restoration" is even compared to the sleep of death when, he believed, the body became a "living soul":

Until, the breath of this corporeal frame
And even the motion of our human blood
Almost suspended, we are laid asleep
In body, and become a living soul:

(Lines 44–47)

Here, surely, we have an echo, albeit in reverse, of the verse in Genesis 2:7: "And the Lord God formed man of the dust of the ground, and breathed into his nostrils the breath of life; and man became a living soul." Wordsworth immediately speaks of the spiritual quality of the Wye landscape:

If this
Be but a vain belief—yet oh, how oft
In darkness, and amid the many shapes
Of joyless daylight, when the fretful stir
Unprofitable, and the fever of the world,
Have hung upon the beatings of my heart,
How oft, in spirit, have I turned to thee,
O sylvan Wye! Thou wanderer through the woods,
How oft has my spirit turned to thee!
(Lines 50–56)

There is another, clearly scriptural thought in lines eighty nine to one hundred, which comes even closer to the inspiration the poet received from nature:

For I have learned
To look on nature not as in the hour
Of thoughtless youth, but hearing oftentimes
The still, sad music of humanity,
Not harsh nor grating, though of ample power
To chasten and subdue. And I have felt
A presence that disturbs me with the joy
Of elevated thoughts, a sense sublime
Of something far more deeply interfused,
Whose dwelling is the light of setting suns,
And the round ocean, and the living air,
And the blue sky, and the mind of man.
(Lines 89–100)

The Bible reference is to the way in which God spoke to Elijah, 1 Kings 19:11–12:

And the angel said, Go forth, and stand upon the mount
before the Lord. And behold, the Lord passed by, and a
great and strong wind rent the mountains, and brake in
pieces the rocks before the Lord: but the Lord was not in the
wind: and after the wind an earthquake; but the Lord was
not in the earthquake: and after the earthquake a fire: but

> *the Lord was not in the fire: and after the fire a still small voice.*

Again, there is an echo of "the still small voice" in this passage and Wordsworth's 'still, sad music of humanity.' There is no mention of God in Wordsworth's poem or in most of his poetry, but the thoughts expressed in "Tintern Abbey" are deeply spiritual. To the poet, nature is able to make the spirit soar and although there is "a presence that disturbs," the result gives to man "elevated thoughts" and a spiritual insight that is both restorative and illuminating. The theme was to be taken up by the American poet, John Greenleaf Whittier (1807–1892) in his poem, "The brewing of Soma," part of which is best known as the hymn, "Dear Lord and Father of mankind," the last verse of which reads:

> *Breathe through the heats of our desire*
> *Thy coolness and thy balm;*
> *Let sense be dumb, let flesh retire;*
> *Speak through the earthquake, wind and fire,*
> *O still small voice of calm!*
> *O still small voice of calm!*

The final section of "Tintern Abbey," from lines one hundred and fifteen to the end, is notable for what it tells us about Wordsworth's relationship with his sister, Dorothy:

> *For thou art with me, here, upon the banks*
> *Of this fair river; thou my dearest Friend,*
> *My dear, dear Friend, and in thy voice I catch*
> *The language of my former heart, and read*
> *My former pleasures in the shooting lights*
> *Of thy wild eyes. Oh! Yet a little while*
> *May I behold in thee what I was once,*
> *My dear, dear Sister! And this prayer I make,*
> *Knowing that Nature never did betray*
> *The heart that loved her; 'tis her privilege,*
> *Through all the years of this our life, to lead*
> *From joy to joy; for she can so inform*
> *The mind that is within us, so impress*
> *With quietness and beauty, and so feed*
> *With lofty thoughts, that neither evil tongues,*

> *Rash judgments, nor the sneers of selfish men,*
> *Nor greetings where no kindness is, not all*
> *The dreary intercourse of daily life,*
> *Shall e'er prevail against us, or disturb*
> *Our cheerful faith that all which we behold*
> *Is full of blessings...*
> (Lines 115–135)
>
> *...Nor perchance,*
> *If I should be where I no more can hear*
> *Thy voice, nor catch from thy wild eyes these gleams*
> *Of past existence—wilt thou then forget*
> *That on the banks of this delightful stream*
> *We stood together; and that I, so long*
> *A worshipper of Nature, hither came,*
> *Unwearied in that service: rather say*
> *With warmer love—Oh! with far deeper zeal*
> *Of holier love. Nor wilt thou then forget,*
> *That after many wanderings, many years*
> *Of absence, these steep woods and lofty cliffs,*
> *And this green pastoral landscape, were to me*
> *More dear, both for themselves, and for thy sake.*
> (Lines 148–161) 1798.

It seems that this poem, as with others by Wordsworth, can be read at several levels, which says much about the poet's view of landscape and its importance to the human experience. At one level, the poet is expressing his simple joy at being back in much-loved countryside; he contrasts the feelings he has at the sight of those "steep and lofty cliffs", "along the 'sylvan Wye! Thou wanderer through the woods," with the less favoured environment of "lonely rooms, and mid the din of towns and cities."

At a deeper level the landscape is appreciated the more because of the presence of his sister, "My dear, dear Friend"; it reminds him of how much he values Dorothy's company and the intellectual and emotional bonds that existed between brother and sister. It is perhaps the most intense description of his deep and abiding love for Dorothy. The presence of such a soul companion seems to endue the landscape with an extra quality that is "more dear, both for themselves, and for thy sake."

The third level of reading this poem is deeper still because the landscape has a spiritual quality that cannot be ignored; the poet is able to look at the scenery "not as in the hour of thoughtless youth," but "with the joy of elevated thoughts." It is not surprising that many see Wordsworth's religious beliefs as a type of Christian Pantheism, believing that God can be identified in nature and the natural world, a case of "Stormy wind fulfilling His word" (Psalm 148:8). Wordsworth came to the Wye as "a worshipper of Nature"; it is as if he were coming into the presence of God, "With warmer love—oh! with far deeper zeal of holier love."

"Tintern Abbey" can be read at these interlinked levels and in this poem we are able to see, so clearly, the essence of Wordsworth's view of nature and landscape; it is the bringing together of all the senses that enables the reader to develop a similar view of the landscape. The spiritual quality of this poem is not to be seen in a narrow Christian view of nature revealing the beauty of Creation, but it does speak to the reader of things beyond our comprehension, opening our eyes to the fact that we are a small part of the natural world, that we are transient and limited by our mortality. These are feelings, which perhaps in the technological world of the twenty-first century, rarely reach up into our consciousness. However, we can still be touched by the beauty of the world around us and reach out to a deeper awareness of 'the joy of elevated thoughts' or as expressed by the Psalmist, David:

> *Such knowledge is too wonderful for me; it is high, I cannot attain unto it.'*
> *(Psalm 139:6)*

Back to the Lake District

To return to the Lake District, after a diversion to the Wye Valley, in which we saw the way in which Wordsworth was able to describe the spirit of a place, it is interesting that Harriet Martineau, who knew Wordsworth, but did not share his desire to keep the area free from mass tourism, had a similar feeling for the spiritual quality of mountain solitude. She published her *Complete Guide to the Lakes* in 1855, which showed her understanding of the natural world, in ways that, incidentally, would not be out of place in a modern textbook on the importance of the high tarns in the water cycle:

> *After rain, if the waters come down all at once, the vales would be flooded—as we see, very inconveniently, by the consequences of improved agricultural drainage. The tarns are a security, as far as they go, and at present the only one. The lower brooks swell after the rain, and pour themselves into the tarns. By the time the streams in the valley are subsiding the upper tarns are full, and begin to overflow; and now the overflow can be received in the valley without injury.*[11]

It is this understanding that underpins the construction of all reservoirs and the importance of dams as a means of flood control; a poignant reminder of the situation in much of Britain in recent years and the suggestion that increased flood events may well worsen as a result of global warming.

Harriet Martineau had a desire, perhaps equal to Wordsworth's view of the area, to present the Lake District as special in a spiritual sense, especially in her description of mountain solitude:

> *Perhaps a heavy buzzard may rise, flapping, from its nest on the moor, or pounce from a crag in the direction of any water-birds that may be about the springs and pools in the hills. There is no other sound, unless it be the hum of the gnats in the hot sunshine. There is an aged man in the district, however, who hears more than this, and sees more than people below would, perhaps imagine. An old shepherd has the charge of four rain gauges that are set up on four ridges—desolate, misty spots, sometimes below and often above the clouds. He visits each once a month, and notes down what these gauges record; and when the tall old man, with his staff, passes out of sight into the cloud, or among the cresting rocks, it is a striking thought that science has set up a tabernacle in these wildernesses, and found a priest among the shepherds; that old man has seen and heard wonderful things—he has trod upon rainbows, and been waited upon by a dim retinue of spectral mists. He has seen the hail and the lightnings go forth as from under his hand,*

and has stood in the sunshine, listening to the thunder growling, and the tempest bursting beneath his feet. He well knows the silence of the hill, and all the solemn ways in which silence is broken. [12]

One thing stands out about Harriet Martineau's writing that is not as true in much of Wordsworth's poetry; she was able to mix science with a more spiritual view of the natural world. On reflecting upon a career in teaching, it seems true that the study of landscape can be a kind of spiritual experience. Poet and geographer can talk to one another, each bringing a particular way of observing the natural world. A geographical study of landscape can instil a sense of wonder in the observer. It may be an idealistic view of the curriculum but there is a sense in which geography has an opportunity of contributing to the spiritual dimension of our learning, by allowing the student, of all ages, to experience a sense of wonder in the beauty of nature and the natural world.

Carter, R. and Bailey, P. (1996) commented on the place of geography in the curriculum:

The one-ness of humanity is the central essence of geography.... Whatever we do is liable to affect somebody else; what others do will almost certainly affect us. This is also a central message of religious education, with which geography...has close and compelling links. [13]

The seventeenth century metaphysical poet, John Donne wrote that:

No man is an island entire of itself; every man is a piece of the continent, a part of the main. If a clod be washed away by the sea, Europe is the less, as well as if a promontory were, as well as if a manor of thy friend's or of thine own were. Any man's death diminishes me, because I am involved in mankind. And therefore never send to know for whom the bell tolls: it tolls for thee [14]

John Donne was putting forward the ideal that humanity is intrinsically linked together and interdependent. Similarly all knowledge and aesthetic experience is part of the whole. If the study of landscape and the poetry it inspires can contribute to a brighter vision of the world around us, then we are on the way towards integration of human knowledge and human experience.

Chapter 7
The Lake District and the Spirit of Place

One of the characteristics of the geography of England is the variety of landscapes; a day's journey by car will almost certainly be through a succession of changes; so much so that Lowenthal, D. and Prince, H. C. (1964) wrote that:

> *Despite industrialisation and the mass circulation of standardised goods and ideas, England remains a country of pays, where one can hardly help being struck by differences in building materials, shapes of houses and fields, ways of material life in general, and that feeling of community, which makes for a heightened sense of locality.*[1]

They pointed out that local societies try to protect a cherished landscape, as for example, the Friends of the Lake District, who denounced a 1948 proposal to construct a dam in Eskdale, in the quieter southwest quarter of the Lake District, as a "nightmarish irruption of concatenated pylons and power stations which would tear out of the Lake District its very heart, those noble and unravished dales, where, by a paradox of geology, there are no lakes, and, where there will be, please God, no reservoirs."

The strength of feeling in such a statement is obvious to all; it shows, in no uncertain way, a desire to protect and preserve a unique landscape. Eskdale is close to the valley of the River Duddon, a similarly unspoilt and remote valley, which is the subject of a series of sonnets by Wordsworth and will be considered in detail in the next chapter.

Lowenthal and Prince (1964) saw places and landscapes linked to people and commented on the associations of place and persons:

> *The English seldom see merely a landscape; they see it as delineated in famous books and paintings. Not only are poets and painters known by their special landscapes, they have made those landscapes their own.*[2]

It is interesting to ask the question as to whether Lowenthal and Prince could say the same about the wilderness landscapes of North America, where it is still possible to appreciate a landscape untouched by human activity, something which cannot now be done in the U. K. or, indeed, most of Western Europe. It is an interesting but difficult exercise to compare our reactions to the national parks of North America and those in the United Kingdom. It is the case, without question, that the national parks in the USA are areas of untouched wilderness where the hand of man has been avoided as much as possible. However, is it not the case that the hand of man enriches our national parks, albeit a restrained hand, and that we can walk in areas where generations of farmers have left their imprint and where the role of farmers will be essential if we are to preserve the beauty of the environment?

There are literary associations with many parts of the country where writers have been inspired by the world about them, and in their writing have described the landscape that forms the background of their work. These are just a few examples of such associations:

Lake District William Wordsworth, Samuel Taylor Coleridge, John Ruskin

- Wild Yorkshire   The Brontes of Haworth
- London   Samuel Pepys and Charles Dickens
- Dorset   Thomas Hardy and William Barnes
- Suffolk   John Constable
- Grantchester   Rupert Brooke.

In every case, it is a question of how unique a place is and how much it needs to be protected. J. K. Knight (1966) coined the word "Geopiety,"[3] which he defined as a sense of thoughtful piety aroused by an awareness of the natural world. At its most intense interpretation, it leads to a bond between human life and a holistic, living earth and the moral duty of reverential environmental conduct. The GAIA philosophy looks at the natural world in a similar way.

Another important step to an understanding of the uniqueness of a place is the work of Yi-Fu Tuan; he described the love of a place as *topophilia*[4] and wrote of a "flood of sentiment experienced in our surroundings when we relax." Similarly, topophilia gestures towards aesthetic, sensual, nostalgic and utopian aspects of geographical awareness and investigation. Topophilia has been described as a "love of place." It is used to describe the strong sense of place or identity among certain peoples. It is in fact a study of environmental perceptions, attitudes and values. It is significant that topophilia usually involves positive emotions but can encompass the whole range of emotions, including fear and dread.

There seems no doubt that when Wordsworth wrote his "Tintern Abbey," he experienced a sense of topophilia:

> *…These beauteous forms,*
> *Through a long absence, have not been to me*
> *As is a landscape to a blind man's eye:*
> *But oft, in lonely rooms, and 'mid the din*
> *Of towns and cities, I have owed to them*
> *In hours of weariness, sensations sweet,*
> *Felt in the blood, and felt along the heart;*
> *And passing even into my purer mind,*
> *With tranquil restoration…*

Wordsworth was the keenest of observers of *place* in the Lake District and the spirit of place shines through so much of his poetry. It is not enough to say that we can still visit places and see them in exactly the same way as Wordsworth; certainly, it is possible to use the 1835 edition of his *Guide to the Lakes* and follow in his footsteps, even though many of the places have changed over the years, a fact that makes the guide so remarkable. However, we are not necessarily seeing places in the same way as Wordsworth saw them because he observed places by means of the eye and his imagination. In the three volumes of *Prose Works of William Wordsworth*, edited by Alexander B. Grosart in 1876, Aubrey de Vere remarked on Wordsworth's way of seeing, quoting the poet:

> *He proceeded to remark that many who could descant with eloquence on Nature cared little for her, and that many more who truly loved her had yet no eye to discern her—which he regarded as a sort of "spiritual discernment." He continues, "Indeed I have hardly ever known any one but myself who had a true eye for Nature, one that thoroughly understood her meanings and her teaching—except one person. There was a young clergyman, called Frederick Faber, who resided at Ambleside. He had not only as good an eye for Nature as I have, but even a better one, and sometimes pointed out to me on the mountains, effects which, with all my experience, I have never detected."[5]*

It is this spiritual discernment that must be remembered when reading any *place* poems of Wordsworth; such poems are to be read at two levels if the reader is to fully engage with the poet. An example of a place seen in this light is found in the sixth "Poem on the Naming of Places." The location is the area of woodland between Grasmere and Rydal Water, known as White Moss Common and Baneriggs. It was a favourite place of Wordsworth and his sister Dorothy, and they called part of the area, "John's Grove," named after their seaman brother, John Wordsworth, who was lost at sea in 1805.

The place is clearly described and yet, the place is made more dear to the poet by the memory of his brother:

> *Thither do I withdraw when cloudless suns*
> *Shine hot, or wind blows troublesome and strong*
> *And there I sit at evening, when the steep*
> *Of Silver-how, and Grasmere's peaceful lake,*
> *And one green island, gleams between the stems*
> *Of the dark firs, a visionary scene!*
> *And while I gaze upon the spectacle*
> *Of clouded splendour, on this dream-like sight*
> *Of solemn loveliness, I think on thee,*
> *My brother, and on all which thou hast lost.*

Dorothy wrote of this scene in her journal entry for Thursday 29th April 1802. It is obvious that the place itself was important to both brother and sister and was where they could stroll in the evening and feel the peace of such a visionary scene. Wordsworth observed the scene with his eye, as we can do ourselves. It was, however, the place where William and Dorothy said goodbye to their brother, John, as he returned to sea for the last time. It was, therefore, always to be a place full of the dearest memories, a place of "solemn loveliness." It reminded Wordsworth of so much, especially after he heard of the loss of his brother in a shipwreck. John was the Commander of the Honourable East India Company's Vessel, the Earl of Abergavenny, which was lost in a shipwreck. The last lines of the poem illustrate, so beautifully, how the place lived in the poet's memory and would always be dear to him, seen with the eye, but in the imagination as well, a memorial to what had been lost. The place was always to remind the poet of his brother and help to recall the pleasant times they had spent together. I am sure we all have special places in our mind that will always be associated with people or events that live in our memories. Such places are special and are seen as sacred in our life, places that are endowed with a spiritual quality. In Wordsworth's case the place is where he could be closest to his brother and there is something of great beauty as he paces up and down in the woods and muses on his brother matching him pace for pace on the deck of his ship:

> *Nor seldom, if I rightly guess, while Thou*
> *Muttering the verses which I muttered first*
> *Among the mountains, through the midnight watch*
> *Art pacing thoughtfully the vessel's deck*
> *In some far region, here, while o'er my head*
> *At every impulse of the moving breeze,*
> *The fir-grove murmers with a sea-like sound,*
> *Alone I tread this path;—for aught I know,*
> *Timing my steps to thine; and, with a store*
> *Of undistinguishable sympathies,*
> *Mingling most earnest wished for the day*
> *When we, and others whom we love, shall meet*
> *A second time, in Grasmere's happy vale.*

After the news of his brother's loss in a shipwreck there was always to be one place where his brother lived in his mind and in his memory.

Place, Landscape and Imagination in the poetry of William Wordsworth.

It has been seen that Wordsworth saw places with his eyes and with his imagination. His love of John's Grove was more than the appreciation of a favourite location, where he found relaxation; the location became a means of reminding him of his brother and acquired a kind of spiritual importance. In terms of Yi-Fu Tuan's topophilia, the place appealed to the emotions of the poet, in a way that was very personal; a nostalgic location which lived in the memory.

It has been suggested that Wordsworth sometimes saw a landscape in a rather sanitised way, so that his view was not a true representation of reality. It may be that we are all capable of seeing landscape in a similar way. We could say that our view is more than the actual view before us, a view that can be captured in a photograph. Our view may be unique to ourselves as it is overlaid by different emotions and memories. Such a view can be described as a very personal view of landscape, a landscape of memory, in our minds, a view that can, perhaps, be described as spiritual.

In the next section of this chapter, several other poems are examined and an attempt is made to see the significance to the poet of location and imagination.

"Michael, A Pastoral Poem"

In an essay on the "Lyrical Ballads," Foakes, R. A. (1999)[6] argues that Wordsworth saw nature as both tamed and wild, savage and cultivated, "grandeur combined with humanising pastoral domesticity." We can still recognise the landscapes in his poetry and it does not really matter if Wordsworth described landscapes, in his memory, which are more beautiful than in reality. He confessed in "Tintern Abbey" that his eye looked on the natural scene and he attached feelings and meanings to what he saw:

> *...For I have learned*
> *To look on nature, not as in the hour*

> *Of thoughtless youth; but hearing oftentimes*
> *The still sad music of humanity...*

In his pastoral poem "Michael," we have an example of how Wordsworth set a poem in a particular location and used the location to say something important about human nature. The poem is set in Greenhead Ghyll, a stream to the northeast of Grasmere that flows into the River Rothay. In the opening lines of the poem, Wordsworth describes the opening out of the valley of this small stream above the waterfalls:

> *If from the public way you turn your steps*
> *Up from the tumultuous brook of Greenhead Ghyll,*
> *You will suppose that with an upright path*
> *Your feet must struggle, in such bold ascent*
> *The pastoral mountains front you, face to face.*
> *But courage! for besides that boisterous brook*
> *The mountains have all opened out themselves,*
> *And made a hidden valley of their own.*
> *(Lines 1–8)*

Wordsworth described a valley and a mountain stream that represented many similar landscapes throughout the Lake District, and yet he managed to place before us a heroic landscape, a setting for the main character, Michael, described in the poem.

We notice the choice of words and phrases he used to describe this landscape: "the tumultuous brook," "an upright path," "in such bold ascent," and "that boisterous brook." The words he used matched the character of the old shepherd, so that landscape and man are seen in unison:

> *Upon the forest-side in Grasmere vale*
> *Here dwelt a shepherd, Michael was his name,*
> *An old man, stout of heart and strong of limb.*
> *His bodily frame had been from youth to age*
> *Of an unusual strength; his mind was keen,*
> *Intense, and frugal, apt for all affairs...*
> *(Lines 40–45)*

It is not just the ruggedness of landscape and shepherd that is here described; we learn a lot about the poet as well:

> *...Beside the brook*
> *There is a straggling heap of unhewn stones;*
> *And to that space a story appertains,*
> *Which, though it be ungarnished with events,*
> *Is not unfit, I deem, for the fireside*
> *Or for the summer shade. It was the first,*
> *The earliest of those tales that spake to me*
> *Of shepherds, dwellers in the valleys, men*
> *Whom I have always loved—not verily*
> *For their own sakes, but for the fields and hills*
> *Where was their occupation and abode.*
> *And hence this tale, while I was but a boy—*
> *Careless of books, yet having felt the power*
> *Of nature—by the gentle agency*
> *Of natural objects let me on to feel*
> *For passions that were not my own, and think*
> *(At random and imperfectly indeed)*
> *Of man, the heart of man, and human life.*
> (Lines 16–33)

In this passage we learn so much about the character of Wordsworth, his love of the landscape and the character of those who made their living on the land. The 1798 and 1800 editions of "Lyrical Ballads" are full of similar characters, men and women such as "Goody Blake and Harry Gill" and "the old Huntsman." Wordsworth's constant thinking "on man, the heart of man, and human life" was to have been the subject of an epic poem, "The Recluse," which was unfinished. We do, however, have the "Prospectus to The Recluse" written in 1799, soon after Wordsworth arrived in Grasmere. In the first few lines of this "Prospectus," we read of the poets intentions:

> *On man, on nature, and on human life,*
> *Thinking in solitude, from time to time*
> *I find sweet passions traversing my soul*
> *Like music; unto these, where'er I may,*
> *I would give utterance in numerous verse.*

"The Recluse" may not have been finished but surely, in so much of his work Wordsworth achieved his ambition.

In the poem "Michael," we have an heroic picture of domesticity in a life of unremitting struggle and hardship. Michael was a yeoman farmer, at the time called a *statesman* farmer. These were usually small, independent farmers making a living from inherited land, living in a small cottage called "Evening Star" together with his wife and son:

> *He had not passed his days in singleness.*
> *He had a Wife, a comely matron, old*
> *Though younger than himself full twenty years.*
> *She was a woman of a stirring life*
> *Whose heart was in her house: two wheels she had*
> *Of antique form, this large for spinning wool,*
> *That small for flax, and if one wheel had rest,*
> *It was because the other was at work.*
> *The Pair had but one Inmate in their house,*
> *An only Child, who had been born to them*
> *When Michael telling o'er his years began*
> *To deem that he was old, in Shepherd's phrase,*
> *With one foot in the grave. This only son,*
> *With two brave sheepdogs tried in many a storm,*
> *The one of an inestimable worth,*
> *Made all their Household. I may truly say,*
> *That they were as a proverb in the vale*
> *For endless industry.*

Wordsworth set the cottage firmly into an identifiable landscape:

> *Their cottage on a plot of rising ground*
> *Stood single, with large prospect North and South,*
> *High into Easedale, up to Dunmail-Raise,*
> *And Westward to the village near the Lake.*
> *And from the constant light so regular*
> *And so far seen, the House itself by all*
> *Who dwelt within the limits of the vale,*
> *Both old and young, was named The Evening Star.*

There is a reconstruction of this simple cottage room in the Wordsworth Museum and Art Gallery at Grasmere.

The old shepherd, at eight-one years of age, was still at one with his work and surroundings, out in weather when most would be indoors:

> *Fields, where with cheerful spirits he had breathed*
> *The common air; hills, which with vigorous step*
> *He had so often climbed; which had impressed*
> *So many incidents upon his mind*
> *Of hardship, skill or courage, joy or fear;*
> *Which, like a book, preserved the memory*
> *Of the dumb animals, whom he had saved,*
> *Had fed or sheltered, linking to such acts*
> *The certainty of honourable gain;*
> *Those fields, those hills—what could they less? had laid*
> *Strong hold on his affections, were to him*
> *A pleasurable feeling of blind love,*
> *The pleasure which there is in life itself.*
> *(Lines 65–77)*

The story told in this poem is a touching one and concerns Luke, a child of the old age of his parents, Michael and Isabel. As the boy grows he is the constant delight and companion of his father, "his comfort and his only hope":

> *But soon as Luke, full ten years old, could stand*
> *Against the mountain blasts; and to the heights,*
> *Not fearing toil, nor length of weary ways,*
> *He with his father daily went, and they*
> *Were as companions, why should I relate*
> *That objects which the Shepherd loved before*
> *Were dearer now? that from the Boy there came*
> *Feelings and emanations—things which were*
> *Light to the sun and music to the wind;*
> *And that the old Man's heart seemed born again?*
> *(Lines 187–196)*

The family fell on bad times and Michael is left with no option but to send his son away, to try and make his fortune; before he goes, Luke lays the corner stone of a sheepfold, as his father hopes that his son will one day return and work the family farm. It is this hope that keeps Michael content as he continues with his work: "with confident and cheerful thoughts." The fact that Luke eventually got into bad company and had to escape the country is the final cause of Michael's distress and eventual death. Wordsworth did not lessen the human tragedy of the story, and as before, the focus is always on the landscape. Michael is still seen at one with the place and his life's work:

> *Among the rocks*
> *He went, and still looked up to sun and cloud,*
> *And listened to the wind; and as before,*
> *Performed all kinds of labour for his sheep,*
> *And for the land, his small inheritance.*
> *(Lines 450–454)*

There is something in this poem that reminds us of the Father and The Prodigal Son, in the Gospels; it is, however, the old shepherd, Michael, and the spirit of the place that remains in the memory, as the poem ends where it began:

> *The Cottage which was named the Evening Star*
> *Is gone—the ploughshare has been through the ground*
> *On which it stood; great changes have been wrought*
> *In all the neighbourhood:—yet the oak is left*
> *That grew beside their door; and the remains*
> *Of the unfinished Sheep-fold may be seen*
> *Beside the boisterous brook of Greenhead Ghyll.*
> *(Lines 471–477)*

"Fidelity"

This poem commemorates the death of Charles Gough in April 1805, who fell from Striding Edge on Helvellyn, above Red Tarn. His body was found three months later, beside his faithful Irish terrier, Foxey, who had remained on guard beside his master. Wordsworth and Walter Scott climbed Helvellyn in October 1805 and Scott also wrote a poem called "Helvellyn."

In Wordsworth's poem "Fidelity" we have the poet's description of a glacial corrie, or cwm:

> *It was a cove, a huge recess,*
> *That keeps, till June, December's snow;*
> *A lofty precipice in front,*
> *A silent tarn below!*

> *Far in the bosom of Helvellyn,*
> *Remote from public road or dwelling,*
> *Pathway, or cultivated land;*
> *From trace of human foot or hand.*

In this poem we are presented, as so often with Wordsworth, with a mixture of landscape moods. We have the remoteness of Red Tarn, the scattered rocks at the foot of the "lofty precipice"; the silence and stillness of the location, far from human habitation; but at the same time, there is the "lonely cheer" at the sight of a leaping fish. Wordsworth was able in a few phrases to give a word picture of this place and, at the same time, to encapsulate so much of Lakeland's appeal:

> *There sometimes does a leaping fish*
> *Send through the tarn a lonely cheer;*
> *The crags repeat the raven's croak,*
> *In symphony austere;*
> *Thither the rainbow comes—the cloud—*
> *And mists that spread the flying shroud;*
> *And sunbeams; and the sounding blast,*
> *That if it could, would hurry past;*
> *But that enormous barrier holds it fast.*

Most visitors to these locations will readily identify with the poet in his description of such rugged grandeur. In a few words, our minds are centred on the human drama of the poem, so starkly presented to the shepherd, as he finds the skeleton, watched over by the faithful dog. The scene is quickly understood by the shepherd, who knew the identity of the fallen and the scene was presented by Wordsworth in words which describe the desolation of the location:

> *From those abrupt and perilous rocks*
> *The man had fallen, that place of fear!*

Wordsworth later described the location as "that savage place!" The poem is one more example of the perception of such landscapes in terms of "mountain gloom" and "mountain glory."

In the last stanza, Wordsworth returned to the purpose of the poem. It is, of course, a poem of place and we can still experience the silence and remoteness of such locations; the main purpose, however, is to

Easedale Beck and Easedale Tarn

Easedale Beck and Easedale Tarn are to the northwest of Grasmere; the waterfall from Easedale Tarn is called Sour Milk Gill, a name which well describes the chaotic descent of a large volume of water, and the valley was described in Wordsworth's first "Poem on the Naming of Places." The poem, written in 1800 is no more than forty-seven lines but shows so many of the characteristics of Wordsworth's *place* poetry; we have accurate landscape description; feelings which arise from the place and which are associated with people encountered in a location; little cameos of rural life and deeper feelings towards places and close friends. It is possible to find all these features in this one poem:

> *It was an April morning; fresh and clear*
> *The Rivulet, delighting in its strength,*
> *Ran with a young man's speed; and yet the voice*
> *Of waters which the winter had supplied*
> *Was softened down into a vernal tone.*
> *The spirit of enjoyment and desire,*
> *And hopes and wishes, from all living things*
> *Went circling, like a multitude of sounds.*
> *The budding groves seemed eager to urge on*
> *The steps of June; as if their various hues*
> *Were only hindrances that stood between*
> *Them and their object: but meanwhile, prevailed*
> *Such an entire contentment in the air*
> *That every naked ash, and tardy tree*
> *Yet leafless, showed as if the countenance*
> *With which it looked on this delightful day*
> *Were native to the summer. —Up the brook*
> *I roamed in the confusion of my heart,*
> *Alive to all things and forgetting all.*
> *At length I to a sudden turning came*
> *In this continuous glen, where down a rock*

The Stream, so ardent in its course before,
Sent forth such sallies of glad sound, that all
Which I till then had heard, appeared the voice
Of common pleasure: beast and bird, the lamb,
The shepherd's dog, the linnet and the thrush
Vied with this waterfall, and made a song,
Which, while I listened, seemed like the wild growth
Or like some natural produce of the air,
That could not cease to be. Green leaves were here:
But 'twas the foliage of the rocks—the birch,
The yew, the holly, and the bright green thorn,
With hanging islands of resplendent furze:
And, on a summit, distant a short space,
By any who should look beyond the dell,
A single mountain-cottage might be seen.
I gazed and gazed, and to myself I said,
"Our thoughts at least are ours; and this wild nook,
My Emma, I will dedicate to thee."
—Soon did the spot become my other home,
My dwelling, and my out-of doors abode.
And, of the Shepherds who have seen me there,
To whom I sometimes in our idle talk
Have told this fancy, two or three, perhaps,
Years after we are gone and in our graves,
When they have cause to speak of this wild place,
May call it by the name of Emma's Dell.

It is interesting and instructive to read such a poem and to use it as a means of getting to know the poet; a series of questions help in this respect:

- Is it possible to visualise this valley from Wordsworth's description?
- What do we know of the poet's frame of mind from reading this poem?
- Can we discern, from this poem, how Wordsworth felt about the Lake District in particular, and nature in general?
- Is this poem an example of Wordsworth's "topophilia," his love of place?

"Ode: The Pass of Kirkstone"

In this poem, written in 1817, we have glimpses of how Wordsworth saw the earth in relation to the work of some of the early geologists. The years from 1810 onwards saw the work of two geologists: Adam Sedgwick (1785–1873) and William Whewell (1774–1866), who were both close friends of Wordsworth. Dennis Dean (1968) concluded a Ph.D. dissertation on Geology and English Literature with these words: "During the Romantic period in England, literary trends influenced geological theorising; geological theories, conversely, influenced literature."[7]

There is evidence in Wordsworth's journals and those of Dorothy Wordsworth that both were aware of the discoveries of the geologists. Many of the geological theories of the day, in those pre-Darwin days, were influenced by the Bible, with Moses being seen as the first writer that looked at the beginning of history. Early geologists were concerned with the creation of the earth, the separation of the land and waters, the great flood of Noah's time and the final days referred to in Revelation. Geology of the time was seen as taking different forms in literature:

- At a simple level there are poems which describe hills, lakes, streams and rocks.
- At an intermediate level are geological poems that deal with specific scenery and attempt to describe its origin.
- At the highest level are poems that include explanations of geologic phenomena, e.g. the origin of springs in James Thompson's "The Seasons."

It is important that we do not approach the geology of the nineteenth century with the thinking of the twenty-first century. It was in the first half of the nineteenth century that the view that the earth was about six thousand years old, first came into question. Similarly, at the same time, it was suggested that the Old Testament record of creation was no more than a compilation of myths written down by Moses; the extent of Noah's flood was also called into question.

The Romantic period was, to an extent, an attempt to reassert the teaching of the religious worldview against the advance of a scientific view. Although these two views need not be mutually exclusive, they often were and today, more often than not, the scientific view is the one adopted by the majority. In Wordsworth's day, the two eminent geologists of the period were convinced that God had created the world with a purpose. Rev. Adam Sedgwick, as a friend of Wordsworth, would have been a source of information concerning the relation of geology and religious belief.

William Whewell was also an influence on Wordsworth's thinking, although Wyatt, John (1995)[8] suggests that Wordsworth was himself an influence on Whewell, in the way he used phrases of the poet in some of his scientific work: the expression of "emotion recollected in tranquillity," "scenes of youth," "haunted me," and "my heart has leapt up" are pure Wordsworth.

The idea that God created the world with a purpose was held by many, especially in the period 1820–1850, and led the way of thinking called Directionalism, which said that geology confirmed Divine Providence and resulted in "an orderly description of landscape." Two other scientific viewpoints were Catastrophism and Diluvialism. Witherick, Michael, Ross, Simon and Small, John (2001) in their *Modern Dictionary of Geography* defined Catastrophism as:

> *The geological concept, widely held up to the beginning of the 19th Century, that the earth's features are the product of sudden catastrophic events, rather than slow processes of crustal movement, weathering, erosion, transportation and deposition acting over long periods of geological time. The Biblical Flood (hence Diluvialism) would have been regarded as the prime example of such a catastrophe.*[9]

Although Catastrophism is now seen as outmoded, it does raise the question as to whether large geological events (such as river floods which occur perhaps once every several hundreds or even thousands of years) produce greater geomorphological changes in the long run than smaller, day-to-day processes.

Other examples of catastrophic events can be suggested: the sudden disappearance of the dinosaurs, or the depletion of upper atmosphere ozone, or the sea level rise as a result of rapid global warming.

Wordsworth's "Ode: The Pass of Kirkstone" is mentioned by Marjorie Hope Nicolson (1959) in her book, *Mountain Gloom and Mountain Glory*. This book, as shown in Chapter 4, records a major change of taste and aesthetic attitudes to mountain landscapes—a shift from mountains being seen as disorderly and worth avoiding, to the Romantic quest for inspiration in lonely mountain regions. Wordsworth was representative of this change and it comes across in many of his poems set in the Lake District and as a result of his 1820 Alpine Tour. In this Ode, Wordsworth described a landscape of desolation after a disaster, very much in line with Catastrophism thinking:

Within the mind strong fancies work,
A deep delight the bosom thrill,
Oft as I pass along the fork
Of these fraternal hills:
Where, save the rugged road, we find
No appanage of human kind,
No hint of man; if stone or rock
Seem not his handy-work to mock
By something cognisably shaped;
Mockery—or model roughly hewn,
And left as if by earthquake strewn,
Or from the Flood escaped:
Altars for Druid service fit;
(But where no fire was ever lit,
Unless the glow-worm to the skies
Thence offer nightly sacrifice)
Wrinkled Egyptian monument;
Green moss-grown tower; or hoary tent;
Tents of a camp that never shall be razed—
On which four thousand years have gazed!

Wordsworth chose this "Ode to Kirkstone Pass" to be the conclusion to the 1835 edition of his *Guide to the Lakes* and it is not difficult to see the reason. In the last chapter of the guide, Wordsworth gave details of excursions in the Ullswater area and described a journey from Grasmere to Ullswater, in changeable weather. It contains descriptions very typical of the Romantic period, with a hint of the picturesque as well:

> *The mists gathered as we went along: but, when we reached the top of Kirkstone, we were glad we had not been discouraged by the apprehension of bad weather. Though not able to see a hundred yards before us, we were more than contented. At such a time, and in such a place, every scattered stone the size of one's head becomes a companion. Near the top of the Pass is the remnant of an old wall, which (magnified, though obscured, by the vapour) might have been taken for a fragment of some monument of ancient grandeur,—yet that same pile of stones we had never before even observed. This situation, it must be allowed, is not favourable to gaity; but a pleasing hurry of spirits accompanies the surprise occasioned by objects transformed, dilated, or distorted, as they are when seen through such a medium. Many of the fragments of rock on the top and slopes of Kirkstone, and of similar places, are fantastic enough in themselves; but the full effect of such impressions can only be had in a state of weather when they are not likely to be sought for.*[10]

As well as displaying some aspects of the picturesque view of place, there are echoes of some of the landscape descriptions in the best known Gothic novel by Ann Radcliffe, *The Mysteries of Udolpho* (1794).[11] In this novel there is a mixing of a sublime view of nature with something far darker. Jane Austin was influenced by the Gothic form when writing *Northanger Abbey*. In *The Mysteries of Udolpho* there is a brooding presence that seems to emanate from the landscape as well as some of the sinister characters in the novel, that charts the life of Emily St. Aubert and her seemingly doomed love for Valancourt. In a passage describing Emily's first glimpse of the Castle of Udolpho there is a mixture of the sublime and the horrific:

> *Emily gazed with melancholy awe upon the castle, which she understood to be Montoni's; for, though it was now lighted up by the setting sun, the gothic greatness of its features, and the mouldering walls of dark grey stone, rendered it a gloomy and sublime object. As she gazed, the light died away on its walls, leaving a melancholy*

purple tint, which spread deeper and deeper, as the thin vapour crept up the mountain, while the battlements above were still tipped with splendour. From those too, the rays soon faded, and the whole edifice was invested with the solemn duskiness of evening. Silent, lonely and sublime, it seemed to stand sovereign of the scene, and to frown defiance on all, who dared to invade its solitary reign.

The first section of Wordsworth's "Ode" clearly describes an undisturbed landscape, or rather a landscape undisturbed by man, a pristine earth. The geological debate of the time involved the age of the earth and the reference in line twenty to "four thousand years" is in keeping with the view that the earth is only six thousand years old. Archbishop Ussher (1581–1656) had fixed the Creation at 4004 B.C. Similarly, the reference to the Flood is in keeping with this chronology. Was Wordsworth seeing this landscape in keeping with the views of Thomas Burnet, an English clergyman, who wrote in 1684, that "the World is a ruin, softened by God's grace…a wrecked vestige of a former Eden"? The geology of Wordsworth's day was trying to explain landscape in an ordered way. In this respect he was in line with modern thinking that landscape is the result of a series of inter-related processes. Adam Sedgwick in describing Wordsworth's poetry said, "no-one has put forth nobler views of the universality of nature's kingdom than yourself."

The other geological concept of the period was *universality* which was defined by Adam Sedgwick, a nineteenth century geologist and friend of Wordsworth, in these words: "All nature bears the imprint of one great Creative mind and all parts of knowledge are, therefore, of one kindred family." To the Victorians, the greatest unity was that of God. Sedgwick and others believed that geology would lead to a confirmation of the accuracy of God's plan. Wordsworth's view of universality applied to the whole of the natural world, in which he saw the work of a Creator. To him it was possible to identify human attributes and feelings in nature; for example, rivers and mountains speak with a human voice. There is a presence in the hills, on the mountain roads and in the waterfalls, even daffodils could "flutter and dance in the breeze." Are these thoughts so very different from the words of David in Psalm 19:

The heavens declare the glory of God;
The skies proclaim the work of his hands.
Day after day they pour forth speech;
Night after night they display knowledge.

Dungeon Ghyll and the Langdales

In his *Guide to the Lakes* Wordsworth hardly mentions Dungeon Ghyll, except to say that it should be seen "if there be time," in travelling back to Ambleside, along Great Langdale. He mentions the Langdale Pikes several times, as well as Stickle Tarn, and yet he wrote a poem called "The Idle Shepherd Boys, or Dungeon Ghyll Force." "Ghyll" is a Cumbrian word for a short, steep and narrow valley, providing a dramatic flow of water over a short distance. "Force" is also a local term for waterfall and many examples are found in the region. Wordsworth described the poem as "A Pastoral," and it certainly begins in that way, with a description of the countryside in May. The first three stanzas do not depict any particular location, and it is only in the last two lines of the third that the location is mentioned:

That plaintiff cry! Which up the hill
Comes from the depth of Dungeon Ghyll.

McCracken, David (1984)[12] raised an interesting point when he suggested that some of the events in this poem were unlikely to have happened at Dungeon Ghyll, but are to be seen as possible in many places in the Lake District. This is no doubt true, but it raises the question, discussed earlier, of how much did Wordsworth, in his poetry, describe accurately, real locations. It could be argued that his poetry is often, initially, derived from a place and, in that sense, starts from his observation of geographic locations. It was then the result of his particular genius that the places became landscapes of his mind; some might also argue that he transformed the location into something more beautiful, more spectacular, or more picturesque than they are in reality. The influence of the "Picturesque Landscape" school on Wordsworth is discussed at the end of this chapter.

In this poem, the "plaintive" cry came from a lamb that had fallen into the stream above Dungeon Ghyll; it had been washed downstream and was now trapped in a pool of water, unable to scramble out. The poem goes on to describe how a passing poet (surely Wordsworth!) rescued the lamb and told the shepherd boys not to neglect their duty. In stanza five we are told the location of this incident:

It was a spot which you may see
If ever you to Langdale go;
Into a chasm a mighty block
Hath fallen, and made a bridge of rock;
The gulf is deep below;
And, in a basin black and small,
Receives a lofty waterfall.

The incident itself is unexceptional and is probably repeated many times each year. The point of interest is the extent to which Wordsworth is accurately describing the location. Here are the last four stanzas:

With staff in hand across the cleft
The challenger pursued his march;
And now, all eyes and feet, hath gained
The middle of the arch.
When list! He hears a piteous moan—
Again! —his heart within him dies—
His pulse is stopped, his breath is lost,
He totters, pallid as a ghost,
And, looking down, espies
A lamb, that in the pool is pent
Within that black and frightful rent.

The lamb had slipped into the stream,
And safe without a bruise or wound
The cataract had borne him down
Into the gulf profound.
His dam had seen him when he fell,
She saw him down the torrent borne,
And, with all a mother's love
She from the lofty rocks above
Sent forth a cry forlorn,
The lamb, still swimming round and round,

Made answer to that plaintive sound.

When he had learnt what thing it was,
That sent this rueful cry; I ween
The boy recovered heart, and told
The sight which he had seen.
Both gladly now deferred their task;
Nor was there wanting other aid—
A poet, one who loves the brooks
Far better than the sages' books,
By chance had whither strayed;
And there the helpless lamb he found
By those huge rocks encompassed round.

He drew it from the troubled pool,
And brought it forth into the light:
The shepherds met him with his charge,
An unexpected sight!
Into their arms the lamb they took,
Whose life and limbs the flood had spared;
Then up the steep they hied,
And placed him at his mother's side;
And gently did the Bard
Those idle Shepherd-boys upbraid,
And bade them better mind their trade.
1800

It is not suggested that this is one of Wordsworth's greatest poems, even though parts of it are similar in language to the Gothic novels that were becoming popular at the time. It is a poem set in a named place and the question is to what extent Wordsworth was describing the actual location?

Location Notes:

Dungeon Ghyll is found on the Ordnance Survey Outdoor Leisure Map 6 at G.R. 2806 and 2906.

Alternatively, in Lakeland Fells Book 3—The Central Fells by A. Wainwright, in Section 7,8 and 9 on Harrison Stickle.

There are several 'place' markers in the poem, which can be identified on a visit to Dungeon Ghyll.

An interesting study of the location is to consider how Wordsworth helps us to feel a sense of place in the poem, as well as the way in which he develops a sense of drama in the incidents in the poem.

Borrowdale

Ann Radcliffe (1764–1823), already mentioned, was an author noted for her Gothic novels, particularly *The Mysteries of Udolpho*. The Gothic novel is characterised by fantastic and supernatural tales, usually set in haunted castles, ruins and wild picturesque landscapes. She was also noted for her descriptions of landscapes, weather and the effects of light. In 1795 she published a guidebook of *A Journey Made in the Summer of 1794*, which took her to Holland, Germany and the Lake District. In a section entitled "The Jaws of Borrowdale," she described her impression of this area to the south of Derwent Water:

> *Dark rocks yawn at its entrance, terrific as the wildness of a maniac, and disclose a narrow pass running up between mountains of granite that are shook into almost every possible form of horror. All above resembles the accumulations of an earthquake—splintered, shattered, piled, amassed. Huge cliffs have rolled down into the glen below, where, however, is still a miniature of the sweetest pastoral beauty on the banks of the River Derwent. But description cannot paint either the wildness of the mountains, or the pastoral and sylvan peace and softness that wind at their base.*[13]

The similarity is striking between the quotation from *The Mysteries of Udolpho* and this description of "The Jaws of Borrowdale". It is yet more evidence that Wordsworth and other poets of the Romantic era were influenced by picturesque and gothic approaches to landscape.

Location Notes:

Borrowdale today is a favourite tourist destination with many people visiting the Bowder Stone, a gigantic erratic, found in Grid Square 2816 (Ordnance Survey Outdoor Leisure Map 4). Visits are combined with a walk (or drive?) from Ashness Bridge (G.S. 2719) to Watendlath Tarn (G.S, 2716).

Despite the popularity of both locations, it is still possible to share the experience described by Ann Radcliffe, particularly if Borrowdade is viewed from above Lodore Falls or Shepherd's Crag (G.S. 2618).

In the context of Chapter 4, "Fearful Landscapes," it is still possible, in bad weather, to identify with Ann Radcliffe and "The Jaws of Borrowdale."

In view of the length and importance of Wordsworth's series of sonnets on "The River Duddon," these will be considered in the next chapter. This chapter concludes with a consideration of "Wordsworth and Picturesque Landscape."

Wordsworth and Picturesque Landscape

In the last chapter of the 1835 edition of *Guide to the Lakes*, Wordsworth describes a journey from Grasmere to Ullswater, over the Kirkstone Pass. The "Ode" describing the journey contains several hints of the picturesque, for example, "every scattered stone the size of one's head becomes a companion" and "the remnant of an old wall, which might have been taken for a fragment of some monument of ancient grandeur."

To what extent, therefore, was Wordsworth influenced by the "Picturesque Landscape School"? Do some of his descriptions of landscapes or places make them seem more beautiful than they are in reality?

Picturesque taste in landscapes or places can be defined as anything that is irregular, complex, intricate or ornate; and a dislike of anything formal, geometric, anticipated, planned or dictated. It can, however, be argued that many picturesque scenes are as planned and contrived as any classical landscape garden. Kenneth MacLean (1970)[14] quoted an essay written by a Dr. Hunter in 1803, in which he described a cottager and his family, living near Tadcaster on the road to York. Enclosure had forced the cottager to leave his plot, (very much a theme which would have interested Wordsworth). A local landowner intervened and had provided land on which he could build a small building, in return for the cottager's labour. Dr. Hunter proposed that such cottages should be provided for labourers:

> *Picturesque cottages might be so disposed around a park, as to ornament and enliven the scenery with much more effect, than those misplaced Gothic castles, and those pigmy models of Grecian temples, that perverted taste is so busy with: but it is the unfortunate principle of ornamental buildings in England, that they should be uninhabited and uninhabitable.*

No doubt Dr. Hunter would not have approved of the landscape gardens at Stourhead, with its temples, rustic cottage and grotto!

It is certainly the case that Ann Radcliffe, the most eminent Gothic novelist, in her description of Borrowdale, to the south of Derwent Water, adopted picturesque language to describe a "fearful" landscape. It is easier to see other poets of the eighteenth century as more obviously picturesque than Wordsworth. John Clare has been described as a picturesque poet. Timothy Brownlow (1983)[15] wrote that if James Thomson was one of the "godfathers" of the picturesque, then John Clare was one of the "godsons."

In John Clare's poem, "After Reading in a Letter Proposals for Building a Cottage," he showed the ability to describe a simple rustic dwelling where home and surroundings are interwoven:

> *Beside a runnel build my shed,*
> *With stubbles covered o'er;*
> *Let broad oaks o'er its chimney spread,*
> *And grass-plats grace the door.*
>
> ....
>
> *Beside the thresholds sods provide,*
> *And build a summer seat;*
> *Plant sweet-briar bushes by its side,*
> *And flowers that blossom sweet.*
>
> *I love the sparrow's ways to watch*
> *Upon the cotter's sheds,*
> *So here and there pull out the thatch'*
> *That they may hide their heads.*
>
> *And as the sweeping swallows stop*
> *Their flights along the green*
> *Leave holes within the chimney-top*

To paste their nest between.

Wordsworth grew up at the end of the eighteenth century when there was a reaction against formal gardens and parkland. William Gilpin (1792)[16] defined "the picturesque" as "a term expressive of that kind of beauty, which is agreeable in a picture." He emphasised roughness as producing variety, similarly with light and shade and colouring. William Knight and Uvedale Price[17] defined picturesque as being founded in nature: "the most effective means of evoking the picturesque are roughness and sudden variation, joined to irregularity." Wordsworth would have known the views of all three men and Uvedale Price was, in fact, a friend.

The fact that William Combe, in 1809, satirized the picturesque, in a book titled *The Tour of Doctor Syntax in Search of the Picturesque*, does not in any way diminish the importance of the picturesque school in viewing nature and landscape.

It is, however, true to say that Wordsworth, while not critical of the picturesque school went beyond it, and in so doing, developed a new way of looking at landscape. Russell Noyes (1973)[18] argued that Wordsworth transcended the limitations of the picturesque and offered to the quickened sensibilities of his readers, various, intimate and subtle interpretations of the natural world. However, the elements of the picturesque are there, especially in the earlier poems. His poetry was always imaginative, based on place, and, at times, he was very influenced by the picturesque. As seen in his 1787 "An Evening Walk":

> *Inverted shrubs, and moss of gloomy green,*
> *Cling from the rocks, with pale wood-weeds between;*
> *And its own twilight softens the whole scene,*
> *Save where aloft the subtle sunbeams shine*
> *On withered briars that o'er the crags recline;*
> *Save where, with sparkling foam, a small cascade*
> *Illumines, from within, the leafy shade;*
> *Beyond, along the vista of a brook,*
> *Where antique roots its bustling course o'erlook*
> *The eye reposes on a secret bridge*
> *Half grey, half shagged with ivy to its ridge;*
> *There, bending o'er the stream, the listless swain*

> *Lingers behind his disappearing wain.*
> *(Lines 59–71)*

It has been argued by R. A. Foakes (1999)[19] that Wordsworth's "Tintern Abbey" conformed to the ideal of the picturesque, where the beautiful was often opposed to the picturesque:

- Symmetry   Gothic architecture
- Regularity   Irregularity
- Neo-classical forms   Old ruins
- Nature tamed   Nature wild

It must, surely, be the case that Wordsworth's development of the picturesque is that he was able to link the two sets of descriptors together, so that landscape can be seen as savage as well as cultivated, nature as tamed but also wild. Nowhere is this more obvious than in "Tintern Abbey" where many elements of the picturesque are present but are also elevated to a level not matched by any other picturesque poet, such as James Thomson and John Clare:

> *The day is come when I again repose*
> *Here, under this dark sycamore, and view*
> *These plots of cottage-ground, these orchard tufts,*
> *Which, at this season, with their unripe fruits,*
> *Among the woods and copses lose themselves,*
> *Nor, with their green and simple hue, disturb*
> *The wild green landscape. Once again I see*
> *These hedge-rows, hardly hedge-rows, little lines*
> *Of sportive wood run wild; these pastoral farms*
> *Green to the very door; and wreathes of smoke*
> *Sent up, in silence, from among the trees,*
> *With some uncertain notice, as might seem,*
> *Of vagrant dwellers in the houseless woods,*
> *Or of some hermit's cave, where by his fire*
> *The hermit sits alone. (Lines 9–23)*

Chapter 8
Lordly and Majestic Duddon

A separate chapter is devoted to the series of thirty-four sonnets, "The River Duddon," that Wordsworth dated as 1820. The reason for separate consideration is, to some extent, because of the length of the work, but a separate chapter was chosen, principally because in this series Wordsworth demonstrated his keen observation and awareness of the spirit of a place.

These thirty-four sonnets were the result of several visits to the Duddon Valley. The River Duddon rises on Wrynose Fell and flows in a southwesterly direction through Seathwaite and Ulpha, flowing into the Irish Sea, beyond Broughton in Furness, at Duddon Sands. The length of the river is little more than fifteen miles but it is typical of many rivers in the region, with a clearly defined upper, middle and lower course. It is an area that, even today, is remote and somewhat inaccessible, at least to the majority of tourists to the Lake District. There is a quietness and feeling of seclusion in the valley, that, even in the western Lakes, makes the Duddon valley special.

It is obvious that Wordsworth viewed the river as a delight. He even compared it to the source of an Alpine river. It is possible that the Duddon was Wordsworth's favourite river and yet it does not really feature in his *Guide to the Lakes*. In some cases it is easy to give the exact location of a sonnet, in other cases it is more difficult. The landscape around the small village of Ulpha in Dunnerdale, is described in the *History and Directory of Furness and Cartmell* in these words:

> Ulpha is rugged, and decidedly alpine in character, though wanting in those features which are so attractive to the tourist.[1]

In planning the series of sonnets, Wordsworth set out to describe the landscape of the valley, from the source of the river in the high fells to its mouth at Duddon Sands. In the context of Wordsworth's understanding of landscape, the series is unique, for all his other work sets out to describe a single location. In this series he sets out to describe a walk along the entire course of the river. It is not possible to picture a precise location in each sonnet, although there is a sense in which the reader follows the series as if on a walk from source to mouth. There is inevitably the challenge to place each sonnet in an exact location. However, in other ways, the reader is invited to discover the spirit of the place, without particular reference to any single location.

Equally expected in Wordsworth's *place* poetry are examples of the effect of a location on the emotions of the poet. Some places in the valley inspired thoughts of higher things and give us a glimpse of the spirituality of the poet's thinking. Other locations reminded the poet of happy times spent with family or friends, the technique Wordsworth used to brilliant effect in his "Tintern Abbey" poem where the location reminded him of visits with his sister, Dorothy.

In so much of Wordsworth's poetry, nature is a living presence and no attempt is made to accurately describe the Duddon's course. The landscape was the stimulus to more elevated thoughts in the poet's mind and who can deny that the same effect can be experienced by the reader. It has been suggested that the river and the poet moved in the same direction from birth to death and the prospect of something infinitely greater, although it is not always possible to comprehend the nature of Wordsworth's Christian faith.

This chapter looks at many of the thirty-four sonnets, in an attempt to experience a little of the effect the Duddon Valley on Wordsworth; every sonnet is not mentioned and other people may choose other sonnets to illustrate the spirit of the place, which is still so obvious at every bend of the river. These thoughts are the result of visiting the valley in late spring and early summer. They are, inevitably, personal reflections and the best way to understand the valley is by a visit, although it is recommended that the visitor start near the source, possibly along Wrynose Bottom or Cockley Beck Bridge (G.R. 246017)

Sonnet 1

The source of the Duddon is high on the Wrynose Fells and, as with most Lakeland rivers, they form from many streams fed by the boggy fells, which even in summer can remain very moist. An easy way to see saturated bog is beside the road at the top of Wrynose Pass, near the Three Shires Stone.

The sonnet suggests a comparison with an Alpine river. The Duddon was Wordsworth's delight, and he expressed his intentions at the outset:

> *Heedless of Alpine torrents thundering*
> *Through ice-built arches radiant as heaven's bow;*
> *I seek the birth-place of a native Stream.*
> *All hail, ye mountains! Hail, thou morning light!*
> *Better to breathe at large on this clear height*
> *Than toil in needless sleep from dream to dream:*
> *Pure flow the verse, pure, vigorous, free and bright,*
> *For Duddon, long-loved Duddon, is my theme.*

Wrynose Bottom is a glacial valley with the classic U-shape and the flow of water, after heavy rain, can certainly be described as a torrent; as with much Lakeland landscape it can be described as alpine in miniature.

Sonnet 2

In this sonnet Wordsworth described his love of the river in summer ("when with heat the valleys faint") and in winter ("Thy handmaid Frost with spangled tissue quaint"). He saw it as a pristine river ("remote from every taint of sordid industry"). He praised its "desolation" and "those mighty forests" and mentioned "paths and alleys roofed with darkest green." Apart from the minor road that passes down Wrynose Bottom, eventually to Duddon Bridge, the valley can still be described as "pristine." Most tourist traffic coming over the Wrynose Pass, reaches Cockley Beck Bridge and turns right to pass over the Hardknott Pass into Eskdale and ultimately to Wastwater. The road down the Duddon valley is empty, even in summer months. Most of the buildings in the valley are farms and agricultural buildings; they and the churches at Seathwaite and Ulpha were there in Wordsworth's time. There is an air of remoteness and below Cockley Beck Bridge; there are paths which run through the wooded sections of the upper course of the river.

Sonnet 3

In this sonnet, Wordsworth argued that such areas and landscapes should remain undeveloped:

> ...so hath Nature lent
> To thy beginning nought that doth present
> Peculiar ground for hope to build upon.

This landscape should be preserved and Wordsworth used an expression that elevated such places to a kind of spiritual importance, as the river is personified:

> Yet thou thyself hast round thee shed a gleam
> Of brilliant moss, instinct with freshness rare;
> Prompt offering to thy Foster-mother, Earth.

Wordsworth's wish has mostly been fulfilled and much of the Duddon Valley above Seathwaite is owned by the National Trust. B.L. Thompson (1946), in a book celebrating the Trust's property in the Lake District, mentioned that in the eighteenth century, outsiders described the upper Duddon as "a melancholy, mountainous and inhospitable tract." He went on to argue that this quality needed to be preserved, in words that summarise one of the vital roles of the National Trust:

> *It is only as the rest of England has become almost too civilised and its inhabitants predominately urban that places of such beauty have become priceless to the community. And if they are priceless they must be preserved.*[2]

Sonnets 4 and 5

The river flows from its mountain source and starts to meander, although still in the upper course. Its banks are places where dwarf willows and ferns grow; the flow is described as "snow-white foam." Some of this section of the valley has been taken for coniferous plantations but deciduous trees are still much in evidence close to the river.

The seclusion of the Duddon Valley led Wordsworth to suggest that only the river itself hears the sounds of the valley; he referred to "sullen moss and craggy mound," "green alders" and "birch trees;" "sheltering pines." And, here in Sonnet 5, we have the first mention of a "cottage rude and dray," where children "sport through the summer day." Today, the first buildings at the head of the river are some cottages at Cockley Beck Bridge one of which is used as a self-catering business.

Sonnet 6 Flowers

In this sonnet, Wordsworth gave a description of gardens along part of the Duddon Valley:

> *...the fragrance which the sundry flowers*
> *Fed by the stream with soft perpetual flowers,*
> *Plenteously yielded to the vagrant breeze.*

The flowers in the valley's gardens are at their best in spring and early summer, when after the daffodils, gardens are full of azaleas and rhododendrons, although some of the most impressive sights at this time of year are the carpets of bluebells found in the deciduous woodlands.

Sonnets 7 and 8

As so often with Wordsworth's poetry, contemplation of a place is tinged with spiritual thoughts. In sonnet 7, he expressed the wish to be one with nature: "Change me, some God, into that breathing rose." The prayer is addressed to "some God" giving credence to the possibility that Wordsworth was more a Christian pantheist than a conventional Christian. This is not the place to discuss the poet's spirituality but it is a fascinating line of enquiry. His desire to be at one with nature was expressed in terms that clearly show his love of the Duddon Valley, as he wished to receive blessings from the Nymph of the river:

> *There are whose calmer mind it would content*
> *To be an unculled floweret of the glen*

*Fearless of plough and scythe; or darkling wren
That tunes on Duddon's banks her slender voice.*

Wordsworth was only the latest of many who have loved the valley and yet suffered in many ways during their life, and yet, the "pellucid Current" (Sonnet 8) of the river was always there to clear the mind and free the spirit:

*Thy function was to heal and restore,
To soothe and cleanse, not madden and pollute!*

We are being reminded of the similar effect of the Wye on a mind disturbed by "darkness and amid the many shapes/Of joyless daylight; When the fretful stir/Unprofitable, and the fever of the world,/Have hung upon the beatings of my heart."

Wordsworth was always able to receive solace from particular places:

*How oft, in spirit, have I turned to thee,
O Sylvan Wye! Thou wanderer through the woods,
How oft has my spirit turned to thee!*

The same was true of many sections of the Duddon Valley, where it is still possible to walk for hours and see very few people. On still days there is a silence in the valley that cannot be found so easily in many other parts of the Lake District.

Sonnet 9 "The Stepping-stones"

At several points on the Duddon there are plank or arched stone bridges, but also sets of stepping-stones. In the ninth sonnet, Wordsworth described a set of these stepping-stones, possibly those close to Dunnerdale Hall. Here the river is now "a Brook of loud and stately march."

Wordsworth hinted at stone banks to the river, constructed to improve water flow, but not at this point, where the stepping-stones allow the river to flow without constraint. At Dunnerdale Hall, the velocity of the river tests both child and old men and is a symbolic reminder of how fast time flies, from birth to death. At times, even in summer after heavy rain, the stepping-stones become submerged and attempts to cross the river become very treacherous. Similarly, in Sonnet 10, the flow is a challenge to a shepherdess trying to reach her lover on the other bank of the river. It is indeed a poem describing young love in all its innocence where uncertainty eventually overcomes all obstacles.

Sonnets 11 and 12

In so much of Wordsworth's poetry, he used places and experiences in the countryside to remind himself of a myriad of emotions and deeply held beliefs. It is almost certain that Sonnet 11 ("The Faery Chasm") and sonnet 12 ("Hints for the Fancy") are describing the Duddon at Birks Bridge. The contrast is clear. In sonnets 9 and 10, the river is seen as "a Brook of loud and stately march"; stepping-stones enabling young children, putting their "budding courage to the proof", to cross the swiftly flowing waters, something not to be attempted by those of "declining manhood." In contrast, the character of the river is very different at Birks Bridge.

In Sonnet 11 there is a description of a steeper gradient on the Duddon, "A sky-blue stone, within this sunless cleft." In Sonnet 12 there is a description of a waterfall and a plunge pool, leading to a gorge. Wordsworth referred to "Niagarus" and "Alpine passes":

> *On, loitering Muse—the swift Stream chides us—on!*
> *Albeit his deep-worn channel doth immure*
> *Objects immense portrayed in miniature,*
> *Wild shapes for many a strange comparison!*

Wordsworth saw such places as reminders of the grandeur of the Alps and his travels in the mountains and, in many ways, he saw Lakeland as a miniature version of the Alps.

Sonnets 13 ("Open prospect") and 14

We see in these two sonnets the changing landscape of the Duddon, as the river moves from its mountain course to the gentler slopes of the middle course, although it still remains a mountain stream. The change is described in Sonnet 13:

> *Hail to the fields—with Dwellings sprinkled o'er,*

*And one small hamlet, under a green hill
Clustering with barn and byre, and spouting mill!*

The reference to a "spouting mill" probably refers to the carding mill on Tarn Beck, built sometime in the 1780s but derelict by 1840. The stones from the mill were used to build a hut to hold a generator for the Newfield Inn, before electricity reached the valley. The only other mills in the valley were the bobbin mills that once existed at Ulpha. *

At Seathwaite, the river has the beginnings of a flood plain and fields are found on both banks, even though Wordsworth begins the sonnet with "O Mountain Stream!" It is still a landscape of "deep solitude" but now we find, from Sonnet 14:

*A field or two of brighter green, or plot
Of tillage-ground, that seemeth like a spot
Of stationary sunshine:*

The river still flows in "fits and starts" and Sonnet 14 ends with another description of solitude, where the river's voice fills the landscape:

*Attended but by thy own voice, save when
The clouds and fowls of the air thy way pursue!*

(* I am indebted to Felicity Hughes of Seathwaite for this information on derelict mills. [3])

Sonnets 15, 16 ("American Tradition") and 17 (Return)

These three sonnets are rather curious in the context of the journey from source to finish of the river. It is almost as if Wordsworth took time, midway through the series, to muse on many things concerning rivers in the landscape. He was thinking of the formation and erosion of river landscapes, at times very slow, and yet he also referred to dramatic changes as a result of volcanic activity:

*Was it by mortals sculptured? —weary slaves
Of slow endeavour! Or abruptly cast
Into rude shape by fire, with roaring blast
Tempestuously let from central caves?*

> *Or fashioned by the turbulence of waves,*
> *Then, when o'er highest hills the Deluge pass'd?*
> *(Sonnet 15)*

The "Deluge" at the end of Sonnet 15 is a reference to the Genesis Flood. Such references were common in the Romantic era, when early geologists were trying to reconcile the Biblical record of Creation with their discoveries in the rock and landscapes. Dean, D. (1968) wrote:

> *During the Romantic period in England, literary trends influenced geological theorising; geological theories, conversely, influenced literature.*[4]

Dean saw geology during this period as taking several forms. At a simple level there are poems that describe hills, lakes, streams and rocks. At an intermediate level there are geological poems that deal with specific scenery and attempt to explain its origin. At the highest level are poems that include explanations of geologic phenomena, as for example, the origin of springs and rivers in James Thomson's "The Seasons".

In Sonnets 15 to 17 of the Duddon series, Wordsworth was operating at the intermediate level, according to Dean's classification, although it is perhaps more accurate to suggest that there are elements of all three forms. An example of the way that literature was influenced by the work of the early geologists is found in the prose works of William Wordsworth, in which he wrote about the vales of the Lake District:

> For they are not formed, as are most of the celebrated Welsh valleys, by an approximation of the sloping bases of the opposite mountains towards each other leaving little more between than a channel for the passage of a hasty river; but the bottom of these valleys is mostly a spacious and gently declining area, apparently level as the floor of a temple, and broken in many cases, by rock and hills which rise up like islands from the plain.[5]

By the standards of physical geographers today, this observation by Wordsworth scarcely begins to explain two types of valley landform. It is, however a valid description, even though it is not accurate in the case of many valleys in Snowdonia or the Lake District. Wordsworth was describing a glacial valley. It illustrates the thinking of the time and Wordsworth was attempting to describe the difference between a

V-shaped valley formed by water and the broad U-shape of a glacial valley. He would have been able to see the similarity between, for example, the Nant Ffrancon valley in Snowdonia and the Langdale valley.

In Sonnet 16, Wordsworth continues his landscape musings with a reference to the Orinoco in Venezuela and a wry comment that the American Indians have a better understanding of rivers, their formation and place in the landscape than the "White Man's" ignorance:

> *Such fruitless questions may not long beguile*
> *Or plague the fancy 'mid the sculptured shows*
> *Conspicuous yet where Oroonoko flows;*
> *There would the Indian answer with a smile*
> *Aimed at the White Man's ignorance the while,*
> *Of the Great waters telling how they rose,*
> *Covered the plains, and, wandering where they chose.*

Here we have an example of the gulf of understanding between those of Wordsworth's generation and the perceived thinking of those in other regions of the world. During the Romantic era, others parts of the world were still seen as exotic, mysterious and, simply, very different.

Similarly, in Sonnet 17, the landscape reminds the poet of the distant past:

> *A Dark plume fetch me from yon blasted yew,*
> *Perched on whose top the Danish Raven croaks;*
> *Aloft, the imperial Bird of Rome invokes*
> *Departed ages...*

A few lines on there is a mention of "that lone Camp on Hardknot's height," a reference to the Roman defensive post of Hardknot Castle, situated above the road which descends from the Hardknot Pass into Eskdale (G.R. 219016).

Sonnet 18 (Seathwaite Chapel)

This is one of the mostly clearly located sites of the Duddon series of sonnets. It is of great interest in one respect. Obviously the chapel represents the changes brought about by the passing of time, as indeed can be said of the river, but the pantheism of Wordsworth's

Christian belief is apparent in the sonnet; he appeals to the "Mother of Love," and it is reasonable to conclude that he meant nature rather than the Virgin Mother and that he saw the river as "Truth's holy lamp":

> *Sacred Religion! "mother of form and fear,"*
> *Dread arbitress of mutable respect,*
> *New rites ordaining when the old are wrecked,*
> *Or cease to please the fickle worshipper;*
> *Mother of Love! (that name best suits thee here)*
> *Mother of Love! for this deep vale, protect*
> *Truth's holy lamp, pure source of bright effect,*
> *Gifted to purge the vapoury atmosphere*
> *That seeks to stifle it…*

The point should not be over stated but there is a possibility that in this sonnet, Wordsworth was perhaps suggesting that the "New rites ordaining when the old are wrecked" is a comment on the failure of traditional Christian worship to see the sacred in the natural world. If nature is the "Sacred Religion" of this sonnet, then the description of it as the "mother of form and fear" makes sense and is in line with the deeply rooted feelings of the poet. The landscape is the result of centuries of change and we view it with a sense of awe, which makes the experience, a form of spiritual worship. There are many other places in Wordsworth's poetry where the landscape is seen in this light.

The mention of a "Gospel Teacher" in this sonnet is a reference to the Reverend Robert Walker, who died aged ninety-two on the 25th June 1802, the sixty-seventh year of his curacy at Seathwaite. The parish-register describes him as "a man singular for his temperance, industry, and integrity" and goes on to compare him to the country parson of Chaucer. At the time he was called "Wonderful Walker." The sonnet ends with a similar comparison found in the work of George Herbert and Oliver Goldsmith.

Sonnet 19 (Tributary Stream)

The location of this sonnet is almost certainly where the Duddon is joined by Tarn Beck (G. R. 225961). Wordsworth describes the dramatic effect of a tributary stream joining a larger river. The Duddon above the confluence with Tarn Beck is fast flowing and boulder strewn, so much so that Wordsworth describes it as "lordly Duddon":

> *My frame hath often trembled with delight*
> *When hope presented some far-distant good,*
> *That seemed from heaven descending like the flood*
> *Of yon pure waters, from their aery height*
> *Hurrying, with lordly Duddon to unite;*

The last two lines are also very descriptive; the tributary joins the Duddon and:

> *Announces to the thirsty fields a boon*
> *Dewy and fresh, till showers again shall fall.*

The Duddon, particularly at this point, has changed little since Wordsworth walked its banks. The scene changes dramatically within a few hundred metres; the rushing torrent of water in the boulder strewn bed of the Duddon, above the stone bridge in the beech wood, is contrasted with the quiet, steady and stately flow of the river after it has been joined by Tarn Beck.

Sonnet 20 (The plain of Donnerdale)

In this sonnet, Wordsworth describes a quieter section of the river, downstream from Seathwaite:

> *...The entrancement that detains*
> *Thy waters, Duddon! 'mid these flowery plains;*
> *The still repose, the liquid lapse serene,*
> *Transferred to bowers imperishably green,*

And then another change of pace as the river enters a rougher part of its course, above Ulpha Bridge; in this sonnet we see the contrasting moods of the river—from still, almost languorous flow, to a quickening of the flow:

> *...a rough course remains.*
> *Rough as the past; where Thou, of placid mien,*
> *Innocuous as a firstling of the flock,*
> *And countenanced like a soft cerulean sky,*
> *Shalt change thy temper; and with many a shock*

Given and received in mutual jeopardy,
Dance, like a Bacchanal, from rock to rock,
Tossing her frantic thyrsus wide and high.

("Thyrsus" is the decorated stag held by Bacchus, the Greek god of wine, music and poetry.)

Sonnet 21

In so much of Wordsworth's poetry, he wrote of happy memories of days spent with friends or family and the location of the poem is given added interest because of such associations. In Sonnet 21, he remembers happy days with friends along the banks of the Duddon. The river triggered his mind to recollect pleasant experiences, a technique used, perhaps to best effect, in his "Tintern Abbey" poem of 1798. It is this comparison that makes this sonnet stand out among the thirty-four in the Duddon series. The reference to "friends and kindred tenderly beloved; some who had early mandates to depart," is particularly poignant and may be a reference to his sailor brother, John, who had drowned in 1805. The sonnet may not be as *located* on the Duddon as others in the series but it is one of the finest and the passing of time is at its heart:

Whence that low voice? —A whisper to the heart,
That told of days long past, when here I roved
With friends and kindred tenderly beloved;
Some who had early mandates to depart,
Yet are allowed to steal my path athwart
By Duddon's side; once more do we unite,
Once more beneath the kind Earth's tranquil light;
And smothered joys into new being start.
From her unworthy seat, the cloudy stall
Of Time, breaks forth triumphant Memory;
Her glistening tresses bound, yet light and free
As golden locks of birch, that rise and fall
On gales that breathe too gently to recall
Aught of the fading year's inclemency!

Sonnets 22–23 continue the theme of the whole series, in that some sonnets can be clearly located to particular places on the Duddon's course, whereas others are reflections on the course of the river from source to the sea. In these more reflective sonnets, the thoughts and emotions of the poet are more significant than the location.

Sonnet 22 (Tradition)

The mention of "some far-distant time" at the opening of this sonnet gives it a rather wistful air, and this is increased by the reference to "Dian's looking glass." The picture is clearly of a deep hidden pool where the crystal clear water reflects the sky as in a mirror. We are perhaps seeing the deep pools below Birks Bridge, where the sides of the small gorge are covered in primroses and wild flowers in April, but the location is not as important as the sight of the river in April, when discharge is high at the end of winter.

Sonnet 23 (Sheep-washing)

In this sonnet, Wordsworth introduced a touch of humour, as shepherd boys, dogs and sheep disturb the silence and stillness of the valley. It is a reminder that this valley, in Wordsworth's day was largely dependent on sheep, and wool was a valuable commodity. There was a carding mill at Duddon Hall (G.R. 194896), dated 1770, and at nearby Logan Beck, a Waulking Mill for the process of waulking, or shrinking the woven cloth before it is made into garments.[6] The atmosphere of the valley is captured as the shepherd boys and their dogs bring the sheep under control:

> *Distant Mountains hear,*
> *Hear and repeat, the turmoil that unites*
> *Clamour of boys with innocent despites*
> *Of barking dogs, and bleatings from strange fear.*

Once again, as with so much of Wordsworth's poetry, the simple pleasures of rustic life are part of the beauty of the location.

Sonnet 24 (The Resting Place)

In Sonnet 24 the scene is surely an early summer afternoon, when the valley is quiet apart from the noise of water:

> *Mid-Noon is past; —upon the sultry mead*
> *No zephyr breathes, no cloud its shadow throws:*
> *If we advance unstrengthened by repose,*
> *Farewell the solace of the vagrant reed!*

The sonnet shows how it is possible to retreat from every day care and find spiritual renewal in quiet places. Wordsworth expresses the mood in typical fashion:

> *Body and mind, from molestation freed.*

Sonnet 25

Sonnet 25 is again very reflective, although, at times, there is a darker emotion being expressed. It is interesting, but not important, to speculate on the identity of "the one for whom my heart shall ever beat with tenderest love." The poet may be referring to his sister, Dorothy, or his wife, Mary; alternatively, his daughter Dora, or even his illegitimate, French daughter, Caroline. As he refers to "rough ways my steps have trod;—too rough and long for her companionship;" it is unlikely to be his sister, Dorothy, for she accompanied her brother on so many long and tiring walks.

The melancholy of the previous sonnet is forgotten in Sonnet 26, as Wordsworth is reminded of that which had always inspired and which was the source of contentment:

> *Return, Content! For fondly I pursued,*
> *Even when a child, the Streams—unheard, unseen;*
> *Through tangled woods, impending rocks between...*

The poet's feelings of oneness with the natural world are never far below the surface in these last sonnets in the Duddon series. Sonnets 27 to 30 cannot be located clearly in the valley, and in Sonnet 30, in particular, it is as if the poet is preparing to leave the valley, full of pleasant memories and the desire to return. It is almost as if Wordsworth is comparing the valley to chosen comrades when separated by time or distance:

> *In vain shall rue the broken intercourse.*
> *Not so with such as loosely wear the chain*
> *That binds them, pleasant River! to thy side:—*

> *Through the rough copse wheel thou with hasty stride;*
> *I choose to saunter o'er the grassy plain,*
> *Sure, when the separation has been tried,*
> *That we, who part in love, shall meet again.*

Although Wordsworth returns to a location in Sonnet 31, his thinking of Ulpha Church is presented as the emotion felt by someone from afar, a consoling thought to calm a fevered mind:

> *The Kirk of Ulpha to the pilgrim's eye*
> *Is welcome as a star, that doth present*
> *Its shining forehead through the peaceful rent*
> *Of a black cloud diffused o'er half the sky:*

Was Wordsworth expressing similar emotions to those found in his "Tintern Abbey" poem seventeen years earlier?

Journeys end is reached in sonnet 32 as the Duddon reaches the sea across Duddon Sands and we have the last words of appreciation of this river, which may be short in length but rich in scenic variety; a river which flows still in a quiet area of the Lake District, visited by few tourists and comparatively unchanged since Wordsworth's day:

> *Where mightiest rivers into powerless sleep*
> *Sink, and forget their nature—now expands*
> *Majestic Duddon, over smooth flat sands*
> *Gliding in silence with unfettered sweep!*
> *Beneath an ampler sky a region wide.*

Could there be a better description of a river reaching its estuary and experiencing the changing tides of Duddon Sands, as the flow becomes absorbed into the vastness of the sea? Is it too fanciful to see in such descriptions an analogy of our lives, from birth through all the variety of life experiences, until, at last, we are overtaken by the vastness of the natural world? These thoughts may be divorced from orthodox Christian belief and may be truer of some other world religions. They do, however, come close to some of Wordsworth's beliefs on birth, life and death, thoughts taken up in Sonnet 34.

Sonnet 34 ("After-Thought")

Everyone who visits the Duddon Valley may view its many different locations in different ways. We may find Wordsworth's experiences in tune with our own or we may experience different emotions. Each one of us has different life experiences, different ways of seeing landscapes and we bring to any location the thoughts and emotions engendered by other places and landscapes. Wordsworth would be the first to encourage us to bring all these different emotions to our contemplation of any place. We need to develop our own sense of place for any location, to allow the place to speak to our innermost thoughts. If we can do this, then we are truly walking in the footsteps of one our greatest poets of place and experience.

Russell Noyes (1973)[7] commented on the "Duddon" sonnets and in doing so made a telling point that applies to much of Wordsworth's poetry:

> *The river has been the traveller's companion through the various stages of life. It is the eternal life force of man's spirit as it emerges from the unknown, runs its earthly course, and merges again with the eternal. It represents the spiritual oneness of Man and Nature, which was, and is, and will abide.*

The last sonnet in the series is, arguably, the best and is almost elegiac in its intensity, as Wordsworth thinks of the Duddon and meditates on time and contrasts the tenuous, fleeting hold we have on life, with the enduring form and function of the river. In this series of sonnets Wordsworth showed that we can view a landscape in purely physical terms but also with imagination and spiritual discernment. Sonnet 34 is another beautiful example of Wordsworth's genius in being able to use a place or view to inspire thoughts of great solemnity and spirituality. The river itself is a spiritual being in the eyes of the poet and Wordsworth was always moved by the spirit of place:

> *I thought of Thee, my partner and my guide,*
> *As being past away. —Vain sympathies!*
> *For, backward, Duddon! as I cast my eyes,*
> *I see what was, and is, and will abide:*

Still glides the Stream, and shall for ever glide;
The Form remains, the Function never dies:
While we, the brave, the mighty, and the wise,
We Men, who in our morn of youth defied
The elements, must vanish; —be it so!
Enough, if something from our hands have power
To live, and act, and serve the future hour;
And if, as toward the silent tomb we go,
Through love, through hope, and faith's transcendent dower,
We feel that we are greater than we know.

Chapter 9
Another Cumbrian Poet

There can be no doubt that William Wordsworth occupies a unique position in the poetry of the Lake District. This dominance is not solely the result of his place poems but it is also the result of his influential *Guide to the Lakes*, the final edition of which was published in 1835. In addition, the journals of his sister, Dorothy, not only provide a valuable background to Wordsworth's writing but also add information and a sense of place to many locations.

It must, however, be remembered that other poets, some contemporaries of William and Dorothy Wordsworth, as well as more modern poets, used the Lake District as a source of inspiration for other place poems. This process has continued to the present day and is the result of the popularity of the region, a popularity that can, to some extent, be traced back to Wordsworth and his contemporaries. This is another example of the way in which he occupies a unique place in the life of the Lake District.

The aim of this chapter is to examine some of the poetry of Norman Nicholson. He can rightly be described as a *Lake* poet and a comparison with William Wordsworth is very instructive, particularly where landscape is described. Norman Nicholson (1914–87) lived in Millom, and in his case it is necessary to venture outside the National Park.

Apart from his poetry, Norman Nicholson wrote several plays, two novels and a guidebook of Cumberland and Westmorland, as well as editing the Penguin *Anthology of Christian Verse*. He combined Christian belief with a love of the Cumbrian landscape and concentrated on some of the lesser-known Cumbrian locations, mainly the coastal strip of West and South Cumberland, from the port of Whitehaven in the north to Millom on the Duddon estuary in the south.

In his poem "To the River Duddon," Norman Nicholson linked himself to the series of sonnets written by Wordsworth and dedicated to the same river. He took up the words of Wordsworth's second sonnet describing the river as a "Child of the clouds, remote from every taint of sordid industry." Norman Nicholson revered the memory of the great poet but in this poem, it is as if he was observing the older poet on the banks of the river and yet claiming to know the river rather more intimately:

> ...Wordsworth wrote:
> *'Remote from every taint of sordid industry.'*
> *But you and I know better, Duddon.*
> *For I, who've lived for nearly thirty years*
> *Upon your shore, have seen the slagbanks slant*
> *Like screes into the sand, and watched the tide*
> *Purple with ore back up the muddy gullies,*
> *And wiped the sinter dust from the farmyard damsons.*
> *A hundred years of floods and rain and wind*
> *Have washed your rocks clear of his words again,*
> *Many of them half-forgotten, brimming the Irish Sea,*
> *But that which Wordsworth knew, even the old man*
> *When poetry had failed like desire, was something*
> *I have yet to learn, and you, Duddon,*
> *Have learned and re-learned to forget and forget again,*
> *Not the radical, the poet and heretic,*
> *To whom the water-forces shouted and the fells*
> *Were like a blackboard for the scrawls of God,*
> *But the old man, inarticulate and humble,*
> *Knew that eternity flows in a mountain beck—*
> *The long chord of the water, the shepherds numerals*
> *That run upstream, through the singing decades of dialect.*[1]

Apart from the reference to the fact that Wordsworth wrote little great poetry during the last thirty years of his life, as well as the allusion to his unconventional Christian belief, Norman Nicholson makes a significant reference to "slagbanks" and the tide "purple with ore," clearly referring to some of the small-scale quarrying of granite and coastal smelting of ore that has taken place in this area in the past; similarly, the reference to the "sinter dust" on farmyard damsons. It may be that some industrial remains were present in Wordsworth's day, even though he ignored the fact, for the poet sometimes described what he saw as the essential beauty of the landscape, as was the case with his "Tintern Abbey" poem, when he completely ignored the coal barges which were a daily sight on the Wye.

However, there may be another reason for Wordsworth ignoring or overlooking such reminders of industrial activity, stemming from the fact that these two poets were writing over one hundred years apart. In Wordsworth's day the Industrial Revolution was in its infancy and the growth of industry was seen as a creeping menace, threatening the countryside and involving the outward migration of many rural workers. At that time industry was not seen simply as a polluting intrusion into the countryside but was seen as the destroyer of rural culture and a whole way of life. Norman Nicholson, writing in the first half of the twentieth century, was able to look back on the industrialisation of England with a very different perspective. The post-industrialisation viewpoint was able to look back on mistakes made and the pollution of many areas. There was, however, the view that industrial relic landscapes had been softened by time and that the effects of industry on such areas as the Lake District was, to a great extent, hidden by landscape restoration and conservation programmes.

Norman Nicholson, in his Duddon poem, pictured Wordsworth as an old man, "inarticulate and humble," who "knew that eternity flows in a mountain beck." In a 1952 broadcast he expressed his admiration of Wordsworth: "It was not the beauty of nature which was Wordsworth's prime concern—not the beauty but the fact, not the spectacle…. He loved his lakes and mountains not just for what they looked like." In this statement and other references, we see that Nicholson's view of nature, particularly landscape and rock, illustrated the permanence of God. His Duddon poem ends with lines which link him to Wordsworth and the underlying belief that nature and landscape, rock and lonely places bear testimony to the work of the Creator—surely a hark-back to the seventeenth century Christian philosopher, John Ray, who wrote, *The Wisdom of God Manifested in the Works of the Creation.*[2]

Norman Nicholson concluded, in reference to Wordsworth:

> *He knew beneath mutation of year and season,*
> *Flood and drought, frost and fire and thunder,*

The frothy blossom on the rowan and the reddening of the berries,
The silt, the sand, the slagbanks and the shingle,
And the wild catastrophes of the breaking mountains,
There stands the base and foot of the living rock,
Thirty thousand feet of solid Cumberland.

Norman Nicholson's descriptions of landscape are clear and precise but he confessed that, unlike Wordsworth, he had not reached the point where the landscape and the people in it became interwoven.

In one poem, "Thomas Gray in Patterdale," Norman Nicholson looked back to the development of the "Picturesque" view of landscape and imagined Thomas Gray using a Claude-glass to view an artistic picture of the landscape of Helvellyn:

I hold Helvellyn in my fingers, here
Ringed in the glass. The clouds are still as paint,
And gills like tucks along the four-inch fells
Slant into neat diagonals. The lake
Is bright as sixpence; and if the wind
Bend back the bracken, it is but as hands
Rub shadows into plush against the pile.

In this poem the landscape is portrayed as if in a picture or photograph. In a biographical study of Nicholson's poetry, Philip Gardner (1973)[3] suggests that the poet saw the landscape in this kind of analytical manner; he quoted from the 1952 broadcast in which Nicholson said that instead of trying to discover the spirit of a place, he tries to look beneath the surface "to the base and root of the living rock":

"View" is a term I do not like. A view is something that takes place in the eye, in the brain. It is an accident, created merely by the position in which the beholder happens to be, merely by the geometrical relationship between the eye and a number of external objects. And I would rather tell you about the rocks which make up the view. For all of it could be explained in terms of the rocks, and the forces which had worked on them.

This approach to landscape observation is one which Wordsworth would have recognised and understood, although it is unlikely he would have been in sympathy with such views. It is much more likely that Wordsworth's "geographic labourer" in his poem, "Written with a slate pencil on a stone, on the side of the mountain of Black Combe" would have seen the view in such a way, for we are told that he:

> *pitched his tent,*
> *With books supplied and instruments of art,*
> *To measure height and distance.*

At the end of the poem, Norman Nicholson mused on what the view would be like without the Claude-glass:

> *What if I listen? What if I learn?*
> *What if I break the glass and turn*
> *And face the objective lake and see*
> *The wide-eyed stranger sky-line look at me?*

One of Norman Nicholson's most evocative poems is "Scarth Gap." Buttermere. Scarth Gap (G.R. 188134) is the top of Scarth Pass, below Hay Stacks, on the path which leads from Buttermere to Ennerdale. He saw the route picked out by stonewalls and followed by sheep and a collection of men and women, all with different lives and thoughts:

> *There is no need to describe the track; a pencil*
> *Drawn diagonally across a slate*
> *Would be more precise than words. Stone wall*
> *Lay ladders of grey against the green; the green*
> *Glissades into the lake.*
> *The pass is known, defined and understood*
> *Not by the eyes but by the feet,*
> *The feet of men and sheep that tread it; the young*
> *Teacher from Cleator Moor, pushing a bike*
> *With a burnish of poetry on the rims;*
> *The girl who is soon to bear a foreigner's child;*
> *The lad who leaves the pit shafts of the Solway*
> *To grope for a brighter fire than coal.*

The poem concludes:

> *A track that the wild herdwicks still will tread*
> *Long years after the makers of tracks are dead.*

148 *Place, Nature and Spirit*

In this simple conclusion, the poet exposed the fact that his prime concern with landscape is that it speaks of the aeons of time represented by the rocks which are the foundation of all landscapes; unlike Wordsworth, who so often saw landscape in terms of the people who inhabited a location or the association of particular people who have shared the landscape with the poet. A consideration of the rocks, the geology of a location merely exposes the transitory nature of man. The lesson Job had to learn, surely has a resonance with anyone who marvels at the timelessness of the earth, as the Lord set before Job a series of questions:

> *Then the Lord answered Job out of the whirlwind, and said, 'Who is this that darkeneth counsel by words without knowledge? Gird up now thy loins like a man; for I will demand of thee, and answer thou Me. Where wast thou when I laid the foundations of the earth? declare, if thou hast understanding. Who hath laid the measures thereof, if thou knowest? Or who hath stretched the line upon it?*
>
> *Whereupon are the foundations thereof fastened? Or who hath laid the corner stone thereof? When the morning stars sang together, and all the sons of God shouted for joy?'*
> *(Job 38:1–7 Authorised Version)*

Arguably, Norman Nicholson's greatest poem, which most clearly illustrates his love of landscape and his firm Christian belief, is "The Seven Rocks," published in 1948. As with so much great poetry, this poem of seven parts has to be read at two different levels, both of which centre on man's intimate connection to the natural world. At one level, the poem presents the seven main rocks of the Lake District and considers them in terms of their geological age, starting from the oldest, of the Ordovician period, to the youngest, of the Permean age. In approximate terms, the Ordovician period was 500 million years before the present and the Permean/Triassic period 280–225 million years before the present. The seven rocks in the poem are as follows:

Skiddaw Slate	Ordovician	500 million years
Scafell Ash	Ordovician	500 million years
Coniston Flag	Silurian	436 million years

Eskdale Granite	Devonian	396 million years
Mountain Limestone	Carboniferous	300 million years
Maryport Coal	Carboniferous	300 million years
St. Bees Sandstone	Permian/Triassic	280–225 million years

At a deeper, spiritual level, the poem is an allegory of the Seven Cardinal Virtues of Christianity. The poem also records the passing of the seasons of the year, from winter to autumn. In other words, time passes at a scale ranging from geological periods to the fragile moments of our human experience. The seasons also remind us of birth, growth to maturity, death and decay.

There is room for giving different labels to the Seven Cardinal Virtues of Christianity, but in essence they consist of four cardinal ethical virtues from Classical Greece, namely temperance, justice, courage and wisdom; added to these are the New Testament virtues, originating from the Apostle Paul's First Epistle to the Corinthians, chapter 13, namely faith, hope and charity (Gr. agapao) or Christian love. Greek philosophers, such as Socrates, Plato and Aristotle argued that it was impossible to possess one virtue without possessing them all. In modern times, the virtues are seen as dispositions rather than skills or capacities.

In "The Seven Rocks" poem, the link to the seven cardinal virtues is, at times, rather tenuous but in all seven sections a link can be seen.

Skiddaw Slate

The opening section represents winter and begins with a description of the countryside as night falls:

> *Night falls white as lime; the sky,*
> *Floury with cloud, reflects the rising glow*
> *Of the cumulus of earth. Only*
> *The seaward side of crags, the under-eaves*
> *Of trees, west looking windows, gates and gables*
> *Unfrilled by snow, holds darkness still:*

This extract shows that Norman Nicholson had a keen eye on the natural world and the link to a cardinal virtue arises out of the landscape of Black Combe (Grid reference 136855):

> ...*Black Combe stands—*
> *A humped white paradox. The rocks*
> *Are older than the snow, older than the mason ice;*
> *Here the river of time in a delta spread*
> *The bulged and buckled mud that heaves us firm*
> *As faith above the misty minutes...*

Norman Nicholson obviously knew the 1813 Wordsworth poem "Written with a slate pencil on a stone, on the side of the mountain of Black Combe" where he described the work of a surveyor ("A Geographic Labourer"). Both poets were aware of the permanence of the mountain and the transitory nature of human life. Wordsworth described the contrast in these words:

> ...*To him was given*
> *Full many a glimpse (but sparingly bestowed*
> *On timid man) of nature's processes*
> *Upon the exalted hills.*

Perhaps it is an indication of the strength of Norman Nicholson's Christian faith that he saw the permanence of slate, one of the oldest rocks in the Lake District, as the rock that best displays faith, the bedrock on which Christian belief stands or falls.

Scafell Ash

The season of spring, in nature and in Christian thinking, is the season of re-birth and new beginnings and this second section of the poem opens with the awakening of the countryside after winter:

> *The skin of the snow*
> *Breaks and wriggles*
> *From the napes of the fells*
> *Like white snakes;*
> *And blue as gentians*
> *The smooth crags shoot*
> *From green sepals*

> *Of grass and moss.*
> *For now, before*
> *Daffodils light*
> *Like a powder fuse*
> *And damsons whitewash*
> *The orchards of the dale,*
> *Now is the time*
> *When the rocks flower*
> *High on their stalks,*
> *When the metal sap*
> *Of bracted craters*
> *Unfolds slowly*
> *In porphyry petals.*

Again, the description of awakening nature shows how sensitive the poet was to the changing seasons, before moving to the cardinal virtue of hope:

> *Hope is not looking*
> *Forward or onward,*
> *Is not of the future.*
> *Only the bone*
> *Can hope; only*
> *The un-closed eye*
> *That learns (still staring)*
> *Never to see.*
> *Therefore hope*
> *Is a theological virtue*
> *And a geological grace,*
> *Felt in the why*
> *And wherefore of a rose,*
> *And when rocks solidify*
> *And the watching sky*
> *Knows the fire's purpose*
> *And the way the water flows.*

The cardinal virtues of faith and hope are firmly based on the Bible, as for example:

> *Now faith is the substance of things hoped for, the evidence of things not seen.*

(Hebrews 11:1)

Coniston Flag

This section ranges from the age of rocks in a quarry, to the search for shelter by Ancient Britons and onto the use of "Kirkby Roundheads" (roofing slates from Kirkby-in-Furness) thus emphasising the link between man and landscape. The virtue of charity (love) as the very rocks provide safe shelter:

> *Sunk like a moletrap in the field,*
> *Turfed with ash and poplar, sealed,*
> *With bramble, strung with rush and ling,*
> *The quarry snares the early spring.*
>
> *..................*
> *The stream divides, the waves obey,*
> *Now charitable in decay;*
> *And children lie in sighing beds—*
> *A river floor above their heads;*
> *Safe in a wood-blue dream each crawls,*
> *An Ancient Briton in mud walls*
>
> *..................*
> *With Kirkby Roundheads on the roof*
> *Purple as polyanthus. Proof*
> *Against the flocking, mid-March weather,*
> *When the wind's wing and the gull's feather,*
> *Fly screaming off the sea together.*

It is as if the whole of nature from our birth to our rest in the grave enfolds us in its loving embrace, as the child in the safety of its bed looks to the ceiling of Coniston Flagstone. We live in the natural world and are part of the cycle of seasons and years, our life being but a moment of time in the history of the world.

Eskdale Granite

This short poem begins in the valley, among meadows and mosses and climbs to the open fells, with a tenuous link to the virtue of fortitude or courage, perhaps arising from the exposed position of the high fells:

The granite pate breaks bare to the sky
Through a tonsure of bracken and bilberry.
The eyes are hollow pots, the ears
Clustered with carbuncles, and in the evening
The warts of stone glow red as pencil ore,
Polished to a jewel, and the bronze brow wears
Green fortitude like verdigris beneath a sleet of years.

Once again the poet mixes the times of the day and the passing of seasons and years.

Mountain Limestone

Norman Nicholson sets this poem in the two estuaries of the Kent and the Duddon and thinks of the virtues of prudence and wisdom. In the section on the Kent estuary, the passing of time is represented by the slow formation of limestone stalactites and the slow growth of coral. Similarly, in the section on the Duddon estuary, time is linked to prudence or wisdom, as rubies and gold are the result of slow distillation. In this fifth section of the poem, Norman Nicholson shows his deep interest in geology. In a review of the poem in November 1954, the Times Literary Supplement noted, "poets of nature are common, but poets of geology are rare indeed." It is also reported by Philip Gardner (1973) in his book on Norman Nicholson, that the poet saw no division between science and poetry: "Science, in fact, instead of destroying my conception of the world enriches and clarifies it, and it is when I have turned to science to help me understand the world around me that I have found much of the material for my poetry.[3]

By the Duddon Estuary
See how the prudent stone,
Secretive sea-beast bone,
Holds in the mould
Rubies and blood-red gold,
Veins of golden blood
Wired below the flood,
Drop by drop the ore
Drips, drips from the shore

Through hollow ribs of rock
Where skeleton fingers lock
Over the paunch of gold,
As a new penny bright
And red as haematite.
Long-shank diviners stand
Prodding and probing the land,
And steel nebs bore
Down to the hoard of ore;
The coffers of the rock
Spring open at the shock,
And a new life is built upon
The buried treasure of the bone.

The poet muses on the slow growth of stalactites and stalagmites, on the slow growth of coral and, once again, the fragile and brief life of us all, surrounded by the comparative permanence of the rocks.

Maryport Coal

In this poem the seasonal year reaches high summer and the poet's geological thinking is of the slow process whereby vegetation, bracken, trees and "plunging ferns" are turned into coal, the "bones of the sun"; the season is characterised by "a froth of elderflower, A fret of blackberries":

Oh merry it was in the greenwood,
All on a summer day,
When the crested sun like a burning bird
Dived through the simmering spray.

The fountains of the plunging ferns
Poured bright fronds on the ground,
And deep in a wave of boiling green
The feathered sun was drowned.

....
Up spake a forest outlaw:
'Let justice now be done—
Under the waves of Inglewood
We'll drag for the bones of the sun.'

*They dragged deep in the fronded sea,
Deep in the rocking land;
They hooked the sun at the ebb of the green
And cast it on the sand.*

*And buds and bells and spikes of flame
Flowered from the black bones' side;
And the seed of the sun burned back to the sun
On the greenwood tide.*

In this most evocative section of the poem, we clearly see the poet linking geology and poetry, in a way that in no way discredits either discipline. It may be stretching the imagination somewhat to see the virtue of justice in this poem, although there is an obvious linkage between our use of the resources nature provides for our benefit and the fact that vegetation decayed and provided a fossil fuel, so that "the seed of the sun burned back to the sun." Is it too much to claim that in terms of justice we have a responsibility to maintain a sustainable relationship in our use of nature's resources, to repay nature's bounty with responsible stewardship? It raises the question as to whether nature has any rights?

St. Bees Sandstone

The final section of "The Seven Rocks" is unlike the rest of the poem in one important respect, in that the poet writes in the first person:

*Across red slabs of rock
I gaze down at the architectural sea. Now
The same sea re-fingers back to sand
That which was made from sand. The stone is grained,
Smooth as walnut turned on a lathe,
Or hollowed in clefts and collars where the pebbles
Shake up and down like marbles in a bottle.
Here the chiselling edges of the waves
Scoop long fluted grooves, and here the spray
Pits and pocks the blocks like rain on snow.*

On reading this poem, a first thought is how inappropriate is the use of the word "architectural" in relation to the sea, which is forever changing and always in motion, in response to wind, currents and tides. It is, however, soon obvious that the poet is thinking of the "fluted grooves" of sand ripples on the sea bed and the slow process of the formation and uplift of sandstone rock. St.Bees sandstone can be seen in buildings along the coastal strip. The last section of "The Seven Rocks" is perhaps the best example of the poet's ability to describe the connection between geology and the natural and human landscape. It is also the section of the poem where the passing of geological time is best described; the cardinal virtue of "temperance" is needed to comprehend both the age of the earth and the short moment of time represented by a human life:

Faith and hope
Are incomprehensible here as a star to a starfish—
Temperance is the one virtue.
To wait, accept,
To let the wind blow over, and the sea
Ebb and return, raise and destroy; only so
Can sky and sea and rock reveal their nature.
The bacillus interprets the sun, and only in life
Can death define its purpose.
The sea
Creeps up the sand and sandstone like a moss;
The crest of the rocks is cracked like a breaking wave,
The land declines again to its old rebirth;
Ashes to ashes, sand to sand.

Norman Nicholson's use of the landscape around Millom is also clearly seen in some of his verse plays. In these he expresses his religious faith by writing plays on Old Testament topics but setting the plays in his part of Cumberland, in similar ways as in the medieval *Mystery Plays*. *The Old Man of the Mountains*, first performed in 1945, is based on incidents in the life of Elijah recorded in the First Book of Kings: the prophecy of drought in Samaria, the miracle of the bin of flour and cruse of oil; Elijah healing the widow's son; his challenge to the prophets of Baal and the return of the rain. Similarly, *A Match for the Devil*, completed in 1955, is based on episodes in the life of the prophet, Hosea. Norman Nicholson's ability to use the landscape of his home as the location of plays on Old Testament subjects is a good illustration of how he saw the land and people of a small area of Cumberland, as a microcosm of the wider world. The similarities to the poetry of William Wordsworth are clear to see, in that both poets use the area and landscape of their home; the one difference between the two poets is that Wordsworth usually saw people in relation to their landscape, whereas Norman Nicholson started from his perception and appreciation of the landscape itself, especially its rocks and landforms.

To the River Duddon

However, in this poem, Norman Nicholson showed that he could write poems that linked landscape and people in a way very similar to that adopted by Wordsworth:

I wonder, Duddon, if you still remember
An oldish man with a nose like a pony's nose,
Broad bones, legs long and lean but strong enough
To carry him over Hard Knott at seventy years of age.
He came to you first as a boy with a fishing-rod
And a hunk of Ann Tyson's bread and cheese in his pocket,
Walking from Hawkshead across Walna Scar;
Then as a middle-aged Rydal landlord,
With a doting sister and a government sinecure,
Who left his verses gummed to your rocks like lichen,
The dry and yellow edges of a once-green spring.
He made a guide-book for you, from your source
There where you bubble through the moss of Wrynose
(Among the ribs of bald and bony fells
With screes scratched in the turf like grey scabs),
And twist and slither under humpbacked bridges—
Built like a child's house from odds and ends
Of stones that lie about the mountain side—
Past Cockley Beck Farm and on to Birk's Bridge,
Where the rocks stride about like legs in armour,
And the steel birches buckle and bounce in the wind
With a crinkle of silver foil in the crisp of the leaves;
On then to Seathwaite, where like a steam-navvy
You shovel and slash your way through the gorge

*By Wallabarrow Crag, broader now
From becks that flow out of black upland tarns
Or ooze through golden saxifrage and the roots of rowans;
Next Ulpha, where a stone dropped from the bridge
Swims like a tadpole down thirty feet of water
Between steep skirting-boards of rock; and thence
You dribble into lower Dunnerdale
Through wet woods and wood-soil and woodland flowers,
Tutson, the St. John's-wort with a single yellow bead,
Marsh marigold, creeping jenny and daffodils;
Here from hazel islands in the late spring
The catkins fall and ride along the stream
Like little yellow weasels, and the soil is loosed
From bulbs of the white lily that smells of garlic,
And dippers rock up and down on wooden legs,
And long-tailed tits are flung through the air like darts;
By Foxfield now you taste the salt of the mouth,
And thrift mingles with the turf, and the heron stands
Watching the wagtails. Wordsworth wrote:
Remote from every taint of sordid industry'.
But you and I know better, Duddon.
For I, who've lived for nearly thirty years
Upon your shore, have seen the slagbanks slant
Like screes into the sand, and watched the tide
Purple with ore back up the muddy gullies,
And wiped the sinter dust from the farmyard damsons.
A hundred years of floods and rain and wind
Have washed your rocks clear of his words again,
Many of them half-forgotten, brimming the Irish Sea,
But that which Wordsworth knew, even the old man
When poetry had failed like desire, was something
I have yet to learn, and you, Duddon,
Have learned and re-learned to forget and forget again.
Not the radical, the poet and heretic,
To whom the water-forces shouted and the fells
Were like a blackboard for the scrawls of God,
But the old man, inarticulate and humble,
Knew that eternity flows in a mountain beck—
The long cord of the water, the shepherd's numerals*

> *That run upstream, through the single decades of dialect.*
> *He knew, beneath mutation of year and season,*
> *Flood and drought, frost and fire and thunder,*
> *The blossom on the rowan and the reddening of the berries,*
> *There stands the base and root of the living rock,*
> *Thirty thousand feet of solid Cumberland.*

There is a biographical element to this poem, that spans Wordsworth's life from his first visits to Duddon as a child, through his middle age as he visited the area with his sister, and finally to his old age as he crossed the Hard Knott Pass into the Duddon valley. The affection that Norman Nicholson felt for Wordsworth is obvious in this poem, and at times it almost seems that the two poets are talking to each other. As with so much of Norman Nicholson's poetry the landscape descriptions are clear and accurate to our eyes today. There is, however, in this poem a difference from much of his poetry, a feature that brings him closer to Wordsworth's view of landscape. Wordsworth always saw the landscape as interwoven with the lives of those people who lived and worked in the landscape, and in this poem Norman Nicholson confessed that he had not yet reached this point of understanding. Is it not possible that Norman Nicholson was working towards a way of writing poetry more in tune with the methods and inspiration of Wordsworth who was so much admired by this twentieth century poet? He wrote in terms of admiration and humility:

> *But that which Wordsworth knew, even the old man*
> *When poetry had failed like desire, was something*
> *I have yet to learn, and you, Duddon,*
> *Have learned and re-learned to forget and forget again.*

There is one thing that marks out Norman Nicholson as a different poet to Wordsworth. In Wordsworth's thirty-four sonnets dedicated to the Duddon there is scarcely a mention of industry in the valley, except a passing reference to a "spouting mill" and the bobbin mills that once were found at Ulpha. It has already been said that in his "Tintern Abbey" poem, Wordsworth made no reference to the coal barges that plied the River Wye.

In his poem "To the River Duddon," Norman Nicholson did not echo Wordsworth's claim that the Duddon valley was "remote from every taint of sordid industry." The reverse is the case and Norman

Nicholson mentioned "the slagbanks slant," "the tide purple with ore back up the muddy gullies" and "wiping the sinter dust from the farmyard damsons."

It should be no surprise that a poet of the twentieth century should be inspired by the works of William Wordsworth. It is surely the case that the way in which Wordsworth viewed the Lake District has remained as an inspiration to all those who love the area, all those who find the mountains, lakes and tarns an inspiration, a place of recreation in the widest sense and an abiding memory that remains in the mind and spirit for the rest of our lives.

Chapter 10
National Parks: The wilderness experience

The use of the term *wilderness* has become quite common in recent years as people are drawn towards areas which are seen as natural or unspoilt, even though many such areas are the historic results of past generations of farming and land use. One geographical dictionary defines wilderness in these words:

> **Wilderness**: *used in conservation to indicate an area left untouched in a natural state, with little or no human control and interference, as, for example, mountains and large areas of desert.... The recreational potential of such areas is being increasingly realized, providing as they do a range of opportunities, from adventure to bird-watching, from camping to exploring, or simply the chance to get away from it all.*
> Michael Witherick, Simon Ross and John Small (2001)[1]

There is, of course, an older use of the term. In Christian thinking, the Authorised Version of the Bible used the word for the area of Judean desert where Jesus was tempted for forty days and forty nights, following His baptism by John the Baptist. John Bunyan used the word to describe the earth in which we live compared to heaven and the future life. Some Christians describe a wilderness experience as a defining moment in the development of their faith, a means by which they become closer to Jesus and are given the time, space and inspiration to follow their calling more closely.

The twentieth century saw the true wilderness areas of the world under threat of development, particularly the increased areas of forestry development. Examples of untouched wilderness areas are still to be found in northern Canada, but even here, the pressure from forestry demand has brought about the increased awareness that such areas need to be protected. Other land use demands come from mining, oilfields, nuclear-waste disposal sites and hydroelectric schemes. As the demand on wilderness areas has increased so has the demand for conservation. Arguably, the one true wilderness area left untouched is Antarctica, where there is an international agreement to prohibit permanent settlement and resource development.

There are, however, an increasing number of geographers and environmentalists who are using the term *wilderness* in other ways, not strictly in the sense of untouched natural landscapes. Areas of rugged landscape are described as wildernesses and such areas are set apart as *heritage sites*, receiving protection from development but managed all the same. In terms of the definition above, they are places where it is possible to "get away from it all." Examples include the defining of parts of Hardy's Wessex, Bronte or Wordsworth country; none of these are true wildernesses but they are set apart as special and therefore in need of protection.

In England very little of the National parks, including the three most recent areas for such protection, the Norfolk Broads, the New Forest in Hampshire and the South Downs, are true wilderness areas, as defined above, but they are areas where the main aim is to control the impact of permitted land uses, such as farming, mineral extraction and tourism. There are, however, wild areas and, with the exception of the Broads, the New Forest and the South Downs, large areas of upland and moor-land come somewhere near to the definition of wilderness areas.

In the 1980s there was a survey of land cover types, where the National Parks were compared to the figures for England and Wales:

	National Parks Area (km^2) %	England and Wales Area (000's km^2) %
Built/developed land	217.8 1.6	13.8 9.2
Agricultural/Cultivated	630.7 4.5	53.4 35.7
Improved Pasture	3958.7 28.3	46.9 31.4
Rough Pasture	1112.6 7.9	8 5.4
Heath-land/Moor-land	5122.7 36.6	12 8
Woodland/Forestry/Coniferous High Forest	921.1 6.6	4.2 2.8
Broadleaf and Mixed Woodland	649.7 4.6	4.2 2.8

Source: Council for National Parks (1980)

If these figures are applied to the Lake District National Park, then the results are very significant. It is not a direct comparison of each category of land use but is very instructive:

Lake District National Park	(Km^2)
Open Country	1032.5
Agricultural Land	768
Coniferous Woodland	108.1
Broadleafed/Mixed Woodland	142.6
Cliff and Foreshore	24.2
Inland water	63.2
Urban Area	18.2
Other (e.g. derelict or transport routes)	135.1
Total	**2291.98**

(North York Moors National Park, Education Service 1998/1999)

Equally interesting are the figures as a percentage of Land Classification for the Lake District National Park:

Land Classification within the Lake District National Park (%)	
Developed Land	2%
Rock and Coastal	3%
Water	4%
Woodland and Forest	12%
Cultivated land	31%
Grassland, Heathland and Moorland	48%

However these figures are viewed, they show that the National Parks contain a far higher percentage of heath-land and moor-land, as well as a very much lower percentage of cultivated land, than the figure for the whole of England and Wales.

It raises the question of why our National Parks are so untypical of the whole country. The first "Ten" National Parks were designated in the 1950s; the Norfolk Broads received their status in 1989 and was the first National Park in lowland England and Wales. It was only in the late 1990s that planning measures were in place to alter the status of the New Forest, and in 2009, the creation of the South Downs National Park. Other areas of lowland England, such as the Isle of Purbeck have not really been considered for National Park status, although the Jurassic coastline of Dorset and Devon has been granted World Heritage status. Is the reason for such discrimination against areas of lowland England perhaps due to the appeal of wilderness areas since the Romantic movement of the first decades of the nineteenth century? Alternatively, it perhaps has something to do with a reaction to the worst excesses of the Industrial Revolution, which affected the north of England far more than southern areas of the country.

In his book, *Fields of Vision*, Stephen Daniels (1993)[2] commented on the view that a change in our perception of landscape took place at the start of the nineteenth century:

Rugged regions like Snowdonia and the Lake District, hitherto avoided by polite society, were packaged as scenic attractions with guide books, marked paths and viewpoints.

There was in essence the beginning of a contrast between the countryside and the new industries, something which continued throughout the century and is, of course, still with us in the twenty-first century. In an interview given in 1978, Tom Stephenson, a leading figure in the Rambler's Association, recalled an opinion he had developed in 1906, when he was thirteen. He had climbed to 1830 feet, to the top of Pendle Hill in Lancashire; to the south he could see the factories of Nelson, Colne and Burnley, in contrast to the view to the north:

It was just wild country, nothing at all. And the great attraction was that so easily you lost any sense of industrialisation or civilisation; you felt you were alone in the world.[3]

This view is one that many today share and it drives the desire of so many to "get away from it all." The National Parks and other similarly protected landscapes cater for this desire to escape into peaceful countryside, coastlines, moorland and mountainous areas.

In 1982, John R. Gold and Jacqueline Burgess introduced the concept of *Valued Environments* as perceived by different people:

It can embrace with equal facility the favoured landscapes of the elite and the unspectacular environments in which most of us live, the enchanted places of childhood and the harsher realities of adult life, the sweeping moor-lands of upland Britain and microcosms of inner city urban environments, the contemporary and the historic, the commonplace and the unique.[4]

Tom Stephenson was describing what he saw as a valued environment, in contrast to the industrial scene of Lancashire. It cannot, however, be concluded that valued environments cannot be found and experienced in cities and urban areas. Even Wordsworth, so much the poet of rural landscape and never happier than in the Lake District, could in September 1802 stand on Westminster Bridge and glory in the scene, in words that are not surpassed by any that he composed for any landscape in the Lake District:

> *Earth has not any thing to show more fair:*
> *Dull would he be of soul who could pass*
> *A sight so touching in its majesty:*
> *This city now doth, like a garment, wear*
> *The beauty of the morning; silent, bare,*
> *Ships, towers, domes, theatres, and temples lie*
> *Open unto the fields, and to the sky;*
> *All bright and glittering in the smokeless air.*
> *Never did sun more beautifully steep*
> *In his first splendour, valley, rock, or hill;*
> *Ne'er saw I, never felt, a calm so deep!*
> *The river glideth at his own sweet will:*
> *Dear God! the very houses seem asleep;*
> *And all that mighty heart is lying still!*

A cynic may say that Wordsworth was viewing London, even in 1802, with rose-coloured spectacles and his thoughts are those of a poet. It certainly is the case that Wordsworth would have found it more difficult to write such a sonnet later in the century, and he would, almost certainly, have responded very differently to areas of London and many of the industrialised cities of the period. The point to be made is that it is possible for people to value different landscapes, for a diverse number of reasons. It is something anyone can do, and the process will expose the underlying environmental values of the beholder.

In contrast to Wordsworth and his sonnet celebrating the glorious view of London from Westminster Bridge, there is an alternative view of the scene by William Blake in his "London" poem of 1794:

> *I wander through each chartered street,*
> *Near where the chartered Thames does flow,*
> *And mark in every face I meet,*

Marks of weakness, marks of woe.

In every cry of every man,
In every infant's cry of fear,
In every voice, in every ban,
The mild-forged manacles I hear:

How the chimney-sweeper's cry
Every blackening Church appals:
And the hapless soldier's sigh
Runs in blood down palace-walls.

But most through midnight streets I hear
How the youthful harlot's curse
Blasts the new-born infant's tear,
And blights with plagues the marriage-hearse.

The difference between both poems is clear to see and the reader needs to examine the evidence before coming to a conclusion. Blake views London with very different eyes to Wordsworth. Unlike Wordsworth, Blake knew London very well, especially those areas that Wordsworth had not experienced. He saw the poverty and hardship of many and wrote of their degradation in the most graphic terms, as seen in this poem, particularly the last stanza. Blake was one of the most visionary poets of the Industrial Revolution. He saw the "dark satanic mills" but dreamed of building the new Jerusalem "in England's green and pleasant land."

In a career teaching geography, including the landscapes of tourist areas, I have used an exercise which I suggest can be very instructive for any lover of landscape enabling us to think about those landscapes we value most highly. Rather than limit this exercise to a Lake District landscape, here is an example from the area to the south of Poole Harbour in Dorset, the area where all my teaching took place and where there are contrasting environments over a relatively confined area.

Environmental Values and Landscapes

The contrast of landscapes on the northern and southern side of Poole Harbour could hardly be greater. To the north is the urban area of Poole, with its high population density, complicated communication network and mix of secondary and tertiary activities, the whole area forming the western extension of the Bournemouth—Poole conurbation.

To the south of Poole Harbour, across the Sandbanks Ferry, you enter the Studland National Nature Reserve, the extensive dune system of Studland Bay, the coniferous forest of Newton and Rempstone Heaths, beyond that the chalk ridge of Ballard and Nine Barrow Down. Much of the area is managed by the National Trust, with its honey pot village of Corfe Castle; beyond the chalk ridge is the Swanage Valley and the limestone of the south Dorset coast, part of the World Heritage Jurassic coastline of southwest England, an area that demands a response from everyone who visits the area.

One of the most important areas within Purbeck is the remaining western sections of Egdon Heath, immortalised in the novels of Thomas Hardy. Since the early nineteenth century, over 80 percent of these heathlands have been lost to forestry, agriculture, army ranges and mineral extraction and building.

The National Trust (2001)[5] maintains that "the quality of the remaining heathland has deteriorated with the decline of traditional management techniques, such as grazing cattle and harvesting gorse and furze. This has meant that bracken, scrub and trees have invaded the heathland."

Although other landscapes of Purbeck are farmed and managed, there is, in contrast to the northern side of Poole Harbour, a sense of remoteness and natural beauty, places where it is still possible to be alone, even in summer.

In a study of such contrasting areas a geography student may well engage in land use mapping or the construction of an Attraction Potential Index. However, there are questions we all may find useful to consider, in an attempt to understand the qualities of a landscape, for example:

- Are there special places, in all areas of the United Kingdom, where it is possible to enjoy the peace of the countryside away from the more obvious signs of human activity? Have such places certain things in common with other areas?
- What qualities of an area or an environment particularly appeal to the individual?

- Is it possible to measure or assess the appeal of certain environments that cause people to describe them as 'valued'?
- Can the same be said of environments described as "Heritage" landscapes or "Areas of Outstanding Natural Beauty"?

Can "Wilderness" be defined?

Few areas of the United Kingdom are untouched by human interference, yet many areas are valued because the mark of human activity is less obvious to the eye. Marion Shoard (1982)[6] tried to identify the conditions for labelling an area as a wilderness. The process is not without complications; for example, many areas of the Weald of Kent and Sussex, together with parts of Essex and Suffolk are remnants of post-glacial forests, some twelve thousand years old; whereas areas of mountain and moorland, described by many as wilderness areas, are only four thousand years old and are the result of forest clearance. Even areas of moorland are to an extent the result of controlled burning and sheep grazing; if such controls are not in place, then moorland will revert to scrub and woodland in the medium term, as is the case with some of the remnants of Hardy's Egdon Heath in Dorset.

Marion Shoard, a writer, lecturer and campaigner on the rural environment, proposed a set of conditions for an area to be described as a wilderness; no one condition is sufficient in itself but a combination of several is more compelling. The conditions proposed are as follows:

Wildness—where the mark of human activity is hidden and where the individual appears small and insignificant:

"The heaven being spread with this pallid screen and the earth with the darkest vegetation, their meeting line at the horizon was clearly marked. In such contrast the heath wore the appearance of an instalment of night which had taken up its place before its astronomical hour was come: darkness had to a great extent arrived hereon, while day stood distinct in the sky.

"In fact, precisely at this transitional point of its nightly roll into darkness the great and particular glory of the Egdon

waste began, and nobody could be said to understand the heath who had not been there at such a time."
(Thomas Hardy—The Return of the Native. 1878)

Openness—often linked to the wilderness aspect of a landscape; as already quoted in chapter 4, Gerald McGuire, spoke of the openness of moorland:
It's almost a religious experience. I talked about the wild open landscape and the sky, and there's a sense of God being there, Who made it all. It's spiritual in a very big way.[7]

Similarly, the reaction of Captain Scott to the openness of the South Pole is legendary: "Great God! This is an awful place."

Asymmetry and homogeneity—where there is no obvious pattern to a landscape but rather simple wide-open spaces, with solitude and silence. Some parts of the high fells in Cumbria could fall into this category, particularly in misty weather when the walker can easily become disorientated due to the "sameness" of the landscape.

Height—some people find lowland heaths less interesting than those in upland areas—it is the difference between the remnants of Hardy's Egdon Heath and the wilder fells of Cumbria. The isolation can be the same but the wilder fells of Cumbria appear to be so much more remote.

Freedom to wander at will—this has always been the demand of all lovers of wild countryside; in an essay of 1937, C.E.M. Joad, an English philosopher who appeared regularly on the B.B.Cs radio programme, *Brain's Trust*, argued that the public should have "the right to roam," consistent, of course, with the maintenance of farm land in good condition. Joad argued *"men and women will only learn to treat nature properly, to be at home in nature, and to make the most of all that nature has to give, if they have access to nature in all her moods."*[8]

Direct action for the right to roam dates from the 1932 mass trespass of Kinder Scout, in the high moorlands of the Peak District, and the demand has been maintained ever since by such organisations as the Rambler's Association. The right to roam forms an important part of the Countryside and Rights of Way Act 2000, which attempts to give the public a new right of access to mountain, moor, heath, down and registered common land. There is a recognition of the needs of landowners and managers:

- The right will not extend to cycling, horse-riding or driving a vehicle.
- Landowners will be allowed to close land up to twenty-eight days each year.
- There will not be access to gardens or parks or to cultivated ground.

The first of these needs is leading to increasing controversy as the use of mountain bikes and the use of off-road four-wheel drive vehicles become more popular. Certainly in the case of four-wheel drive vehicles and quad-bikes there is the risk of severe erosion to tracks and bridle-ways.

The absence of human handiwork—even though very few areas are entirely free of the effect of human activity.

These then are the main conditions for an area to be described as a "wilderness." However, Marion Shoard added three other secondary conditions for such a designation:

Relics of ancient man—this has always been the appeal of such sites as Stonehenge and Avebury in Wiltshire and Castlerigg in Cumbria. The arguments being put forward by the National Trust and English Heritage for a two and a half mile tunnel for the A 303 in order to return Stonehenge and associated burial mounds to quiet and peaceful conditions is an example of the need to separate such locations from modern development.

Wind—as for example, in these stanzas written by Anne Bronte in 1836:

For long ago I loved to lie
Upon the pathless moor,
To hear the wild wind rushing by
With never ceasing roar.

Its sound was music then to me,
Its wild and lofty voice
Made my heart beat exultingly
And my whole soul rejoice.[9]

The appreciation of landscape is usually understood in terms of sight but the sense of hearing is also important. Anne Bronte in hearing the wind's "wild and lofty voice" and appreciating its music was doing what we can all do and it adds a new dimension to our appreciation of landscape. Listen, for example, to the sound of the wind through different types of grasses or through the branches of trees in different seasons of the year, similarly, the sound of the wind over open moorland or exposed coastline.

Finally, Marion Shroard includes:

> ***The absence of unsympathetic people***—*covering a range of intrusive behaviour ranging from litter in beautiful places or the uncontrolled use of radios in open spaces.*

A more formal way of assessing landscape quality is the construction of an Attraction Potential Index in an attempt to score a series of bi-polar pairs. Examples of such pairs could be:

Wilderness / Tamed landscape
Openness / Sheltered area
Asymmetry / Symmetry
High land / Low land
Free access / Restricted access
Few signs / Many signs of human activity
Exposed to / Sheltered from extreme weather

Other pairings of opposites can be devised but it must be remembered that such an exercise is subjective and will involve value judgements on behalf of the individual. There is, however, nothing wrong with such judgements, for the appreciation of landscape is intensely personal. It is the reason why some people are attuned to the landscape poetry of Wordsworth as he described the Lake District, whereas others find little that is appealing in either the poetry or the landscape.

Seven of England's National Parks contain extensive areas of moorland, as well as mountains and clifftops, and yet, a 1971 survey conducted by the *Geographical Magazine*[10] asked readers to name those areas which they thought should be National Parks. The results were revealing and the following areas were put in this rank order:

Cotswolds
South Downs
New Forest
Norfolk Broads

Dorset coast
Chilterns
Weald of Kent and Sussex
North Downs of Kent and Surrey

The landscape of these eight areas is outstanding in many ways but the significant result of the survey, is the desire of the public to have some National Parks in southern lowland England. Since 1971, the New Forest and the Norfolk Broads have enjoyed protected status and development and exploitation was controlled. The New Forest National Park came into existence in 2005. In addition, in 2004, a public enquiry was set up to examine the possibility of establishing a South Downs National Park. This has become England's newest National Park and was designated as such in 2009.

The fact remains that the above areas were not considered in the first wave of National Parks because opinion in the period from the 1930s to the 1950s, possibly influenced by the National Parks in North America, thought that all National Parks should be wild, desolate landscapes that can, most closely, be described as wilderness areas, areas where mountains, lakes and changing seasons show nature in all her moods:

> *And now I am a Cumbrian mountaineer;*
> *Their wintry garment of unsullied snow*
> *The mountains have put on, the heavens are clear,*
> *And yon dark lake spreads silently below;*
> *Who sees them only in their summer hour*
> *Sees but their beauty half, and knows not half their power.*
> *Robert Southey: Skiddaw and Derwentwater.*

Chapter 11
Past, Present and Future

Ever since William Wordsworth protested against the arrival of the railway at Windermere there has scarcely been a time when the conservation of Lakeland has not been an issue of concern. His clarion call in his sonnet, "On the Projected Kendal and Windermere Railway" may seem somewhat overstated to twenty-first century ears, but there have been echoes of his concern ever since in many different ways:

> *Is then no nook of English ground secure*
> *From rash assault?* [1]

The very fact that there is a Lake District National Park Authority, or a support group of Friends of the Lake District National Park, as well as the conservation role of the National Trust, is evidence enough of the present and future need for conservation in the region. It is a measure of Wordsworth's foresight that some of today's concerns were the subject of his consideration, although no one in the early nineteenth century could have envisaged the impact of mass tourism on the Lake District and other National Parks. There are four issues of concern that need careful conservation and land management today and into the future:

- Hill farming and the role of farmers in the conservation of the Cumbrian landscape; the control of forestry within the National Park,
- The impact of tourism on the region and the particular pressures on honey-pot locations,
- Types of environmental management in heritage locations,

- The importance of semi-wilderness landscapes in a country that is increasingly urbanised, and where open moorland and mountainous scenery is seen, by many, as a source of recreation in the widest sense and a means of lifting the human spirit.

Forestry in the Lake District National Park

In the third section of his *Guide to the Lakes* dated 1835, William Wordsworth was very critical of the introduction of coniferous forests into parts of the Lake District. He did not deny that there was a place for coniferous plantations on a commercial scale but was concerned that controls should be exercised on their spatial development. It has to be said that some people today say that to walk in or near such plantations, especially in winter where hoar frost transforms such trees into a winter wonderland, can be an uplifting experience and a contrast to the barrenness of deciduous woodland in winter. As so often in landscape appreciation, the perception of the individual needs to be considered. Wordsworth's criticism was that he disagreed with the location of such plantations, especially where they resulted in the destruction of deciduous trees:

> *To those who plant for profit, and are thrusting every other tree out of the way, to make way for their favourite, the larch, I would utter first a regret, that they should have selected these lovely vales for their vegetable manufactory, when there is so much barren and irreclaimable land in the neighbouring moors, and in many other parts of the island (i.e. Great Britain), which might have been had for this purpose at a far cheaper rate.* [2]

His comments are understandable in the context in which they were made but some today would take issue on the loss of open moorland to coniferous plantations. Wordsworth was concerned that coniferous trees were being grown in the valleys where soil is most fertile; he contrasted this with the practice in Scotland at the time "where planting is much better understood, and carried on upon an incomparably larger scale than among us, good soil and sheltered situations are appropriated to the oak, the ash, and other deciduous trees; and the larch is now generally confined to barren and exposed ground." [3]

Wordsworth was not totally opposed to the planting of any conifers at low levels in the Lake District and even suggested that Scotch firs, when fully grown, enhanced the grounds of large houses, especially when mixed among sycamore trees. His objection was to the wholesale planting of conifers on a hillside. He argued that in nature woods and forests on hillsides grew in such a way that as land became more exposed on the top of hills and at higher altitudes, trees become more scattered:

> *As vegetation ascends, the winds begin also to bear their part in moulding the forms of the trees; but, thus mutually protected, trees, though not of the hardiest kind, are able to climb high up the mountains. Gradually, however, by the quality of the ground, and by increasing exposure, a stop is put to their ascent; the hardy trees only are left; those also, by little and little, give way—and a wild and irregular boundary is established, gracing in its outline, and never contemplated without some feeling, more or less distinct, of the powers of Nature by which it is imposed.* [4]

These observations add more credence to the view that Wordsworth, in saying that the Lake District was "a sort of national property, in which every man has a right and interest who has an eye to perceive and a heart to enjoy,"[5] held views that were to form the basis on which the National Trust was formed in 1895. In the centenary book by Merlin Waterson, the contribution of Wordsworth is celebrated: "Wordsworth's response to natural scenery, his respect for ordinary country people and insistence on the right to roam the hills which is implicit in *The Prelude*, all helped to shape the Trust's philosophy."[6]

The Prelude (1805 text) Book First—Introduction—Childhood and School-time:

> *O there is blessing in this gentle breeze*
> *That blows from the green fields and from the clouds*
> *And from the sky: it beats against my cheek,*
> *And seems half-conscious of the joy it gives.*
> *Oh welcome messenger! Oh welcome friend!*
> *A captive greets thee, coming from a house*
> *Of bondage, from yon city's wall set free,*

A prison where he hath been long immured.
Now I am free, enfranchised and at large,
May fix my habitation where I will.
What dwelling shall receive me? in what vale
Shall be my harbour? Underneath what grove
Shall I take up my home? And what sweet stream
Shall with its murmurs lull me to my rest?
The earth is all before me. With a heart
Joyous, nor scared at its own liberty,
I look about; and should the guide I choose
Be nothing more than a wandering cloud,
I cannot miss my way. I breathe again!

In modern times, the area of forest inside the Lake District National Park is quite significant. The Forestry Commission own almost 6 percent of the National park, managed by Forest Enterprise and ranging from semi-natural broadleaved woodland to totally coniferous forest. In addition, the National Trust own about 25 percent of the National park, some of which consists of areas of ancient woodland and broadleaved forest.[7] In total, there are 10,814 hectares of coniferous woodland in the Lake District National Park. The Forestry Commission has two functions laid down by the Forestry Act of 1967: to be a Forestry Authority and a Forestry Enterprise. As Forestry Authority it seeks to advance knowledge and understanding of forestry and the importance of trees in the countryside, as well as promoting good forestry practice. As Forestry Enterprise its objectives include the management of its estates economically and efficiently as well as protecting and enhancing the environment and providing recreational facilities.[8]

Inevitably, there are times when the balance between the interests of forestry and the environment is disturbed, just as there are tensions between farming and the environment, for example, the use of herbicides and pesticides, or the "right to roam" in the countryside. Such tensions cannot be entirely eliminated and it is becoming increasingly apparent to government, that farmers and foresters are custodians of the environment, especially in the national parks. This responsibility has always existed in the countryside but has not always been recognised by government and decision makers.

Some of today's criticisms of coniferous plantations are echoes of Wordsworth's concern at early attempts to develop forests at low levels and in the valleys. He was the first to highlight the need to make plantations visually appealing and that all plantations should have a wild and irregular boundary rather than to be seen as straight lines on the landscape, which is not the case with areas of natural vegetation. Regular planting, especially at the edges of plantations, leave a visual scar on the landscape and seem worse because plantations are often located on areas of fell-side and can dominate the view.

Fortunately the Forestry Commission have adopted policies to enhance the landscape, by blending into the landscape, as far as possible, any new coniferous plantations. The policy consists of five initiatives:

- The range of age and categories of species within forests is extended to provide diversity. Over time it is, therefore, possible to avoid having all forests maturing at the same time, as a continuous policy of planting and harvesting ensures variety in the landscape. The introduction of some deciduous species has a similar effect in introducing variety.
- Boundaries of all new forests are planted to avoid straight edges and ensure that they follow natural contours in the landscape.
- Similarly, it is possible to avoid planting on summit ridges, crags along river courses and gullies. The policy is always to avoid 'covering' significant features of the landscape.
- Broadleaved trees are only planted along the edges of coniferous plantations but can be introduced within such plantations.
- In planting new areas of forest, irregular ploughlines are used as much as is possible. [9]

Wild Ennerdale

William Gell, writing about his tour of the Lakes in 1797 [10] described his first view of Ennerdale, in romantic terms:

> *The day after, we visited Ennerdale Water over five miles of fells and bogs. A mist prevented us from seeing the lake*

for some time but on clearing up, a fine piece of water and rude fell on the opposite shore rewarded us for our trouble.

Three years later in 1800, Wordsworth set his poem, "The Brothers" in the Ennerdale Valley. He wrote of the valley in the first section of his "Descriptions of the Scenery of the Lakes" and described "its lake of bold and somewhat savage shores."[11] In 1800 he wrote his poem "The Brothers" which was based on the death of a shepherd, one of two brothers, who lost his life on the slopes of Pillar.

The surviving brother, returned from the sea, speaks to the local priest about the valley and his brother, without giving away the cause of his interest. The surviving brother returns to the valley and is immediately reminded of his lost brother:

*It was not long ere Leonard reached a grove
That overhung the road: he there stopped short,
And, sitting down beneath the trees, reviewed
All that the Priest had said: his early years
Were with him: —his long absence, his cherished hopes,
And thoughts which had been his an hour before,
All pressed on him with such a weight, that now,
This vale where he had been so happy, seemed
A place in which he could not bear to live:* [12]

It is interesting to speculate how Wordsworth would have reacted to the afforestation of much of the Ennerdale Valley during the last one hundred years. Similarly, would he have approved of the radical plans for the valley under the Wild Ennerdale Partnership. This is a partnership between United Utilities, the National Trust and the Forestry Commission, set up in 2000 with a number of overall objectives, amongst which are:

- To develop Ennerdale Valley as a unique wild place allowing natural forces to become dominant in the shaping of the landscape and the ecology.
- To ensure that the Pillar and Ennerdale fells SSSI is in keeping with national targets.
- To achieve integrated land management for the whole of the Ennerdale Valley.[13]

The Wild Ennerdale Project describes the sense of wildness visitors experience in the valley and the degree to which natural processes influence the environment. The sense of wildness is heightened by the relative isolation of the Ennerdale Valley, far from more easily visited areas of the Lake District. In this respect the choice of this valley as a wild place is a good decision as it is a relatively unpopulated landscape.

In a review of the objectives of the Wild Ennerdale Partnership, an article by the National Trust reviewed the history of man's dealings within the valley, including charcoal burning, shepherding and mining. It went on to describe the forestry enterprises in the valley:

> *The woods were farmed much like wheat or barley are farmed, with serried ranks of conifers planted for timber in case of a war. Straight lines, everywhere.* [14]

The Partnership has embarked on an experiment that will take many years to yield results. The property manager commented, as reported in the National Trust Magazine for Summer 2004:

> *Nature hates straight lines. One morning, looking at the scarred dividing line scoured out across the hills by the cyclical felling of the farmed Sitka spruce, he questioned the devastation. People in the countryside like to be in control. But I just wondered what it would be like if we stepped back and allowed nature a greater hand in the landscape.* [15]

The valley will, therefore, be allowed to run wild. Seed-bearing conifers will be cut down and deciduous trees planted. The whole project will take decades to show any signs of success and there may be unintended results to face in future years. However, it is more than likely that the Partnership's objectives would have met with the approval of William Wordsworth. It is very likely that he would have approved of such an ambitious scheme that will take decades to complete. Reference has already been made to Wordsworth's view of coniferous trees in the Lake District. In the 1835 edition of his *Guide to the Lakes*, he gave a description of how he perceived the Ennerdale landscape that contains no reference to forests and highlights the particular attraction of the mountainous landscape:

Such, concisely given, is the general topographical view of the country of the Lakes in the north of England; and it may be observed, that from the circumference to the centre, that is, from the sea or plain country to the mountain stations specified, there is—in the several ridges that enclose these vales, and divide them from each other, I mean in the forms and surfaces, first of the swelling grounds, next of the hills and rocks, and lastly of the mountains—an ascent of almost regular gradation, from elegance and richness, to the highest point of grandeur and sublimity. It follows therefore from this, first, that these rocks, hills and mountains, must present themselves to view in stages rising above each other, the mountains clustering together towards the central point; and next, that an observer familiar with the several vales, must, from their various position in relation to the sun, have had before his eyes every possible embellishment of beauty, dignity, and splendour, which light and shadow can bestow upon objects, so diversified.[16]

These words show that, first, Wordsworth was describing the physical geography of the Lake District, where a radial system of drainage produces a series of valleys, some containing lakes, that radiate out from the centre like the spokes of a wheel. The passage shows, secondly, that Wordsworth considered it important that the valleys are seen from the mountains and the slopes and mountains from the valleys. The Wild Ennerdale initiative would surely have met with his approval, as the plan will bring these results but over many years.

Hill Farming and the conservation of the landscape

In the 1835 edition of his *Guide to the Lakes*, William Wordsworth described a farming landscape we can easily recognise today. He was referring to the last thirty years of the eighteenth century and the first thirty years of the nineteenth century and was describing changes in farming practices and their effect on the farming landscape. In its essentials his view has remained fairly static for two hundred years:

> *Corn was grown in these vales, through which no carriage-road had yet been made, sufficient on each estate to furnish bread for each family, and no more; notwithstanding the union of several tenements, the possessions of each inhabitant still being small, in the same field was seen an intermixture of different crops; and the plough was interrupted by little rocks, mostly overgrown with wood, or by spongy places, which the tiller of the soil had neither leisure nor capital to convert into firm land. The storms and moisture of the climate induced them to sprinkle their upland property with outhouses of native stone, as places of shelter for their sheep, where, in tempestuous weather, food was distributed to them. Every family spun from their own flock the wool with which it was clothed; a weaver was here and there among them; and the rest of their wants was supplied by the produce of the yarn, which they carded and spun in their own houses, and carried to market, either under their arms, or more frequently on pack-horses, a small train taking their weekly production down the valley, or over the mountains to the most commodious town.* [17]

In the same reference, Wordsworth mentioned the receding native forest, which was part of the evolution of the landscape we know today. Although the rural economy, involving spinning and weaving, described by Wordsworth has largely disappeared, the landscape is familiar. We can still recognise the outcrops of rock in the valleys that makes cultivation so difficult, as well as the "spongy" areas where cultivation was not possible. The weather is still responsible for the marginality of the area, and, at Hartsop, can be found some seventeenth century farm buildings and cottages, some with spinning galleries.

Elsewhere in his *Guide,* Wordsworth described the end of Spring, as "especially interesting":

> *I mean the practice of bringing down the ewes from the mountains to yean (to lamb) in the valleys and enclosed grounds. The herbage being thus cropped as it springs, that first tender emerald green of the season, which would*

otherwise have lasted little more than a fortnight, is prolonged in the pastures and meadows for many weeks; while they are further enlivened by the multitude of lambs bleating and skipping about. These sportive creatures, as they gather strength, are turned out upon the open mountains, and with their slender limbs, their snow-white colour, and their wild and light motions, beautifully accord or contrast with the rocks and lawns, upon which they must now begin to seek their food.[18]

Cumbrian Hill Farming: marginal or lost?

Few people will disagree that farmers are a critical part of landscape conservation and that the Lakeland landscape, that draws millions of tourists to the area, would look very different without the work of decades of hill farming. Farming is a fundamental component of the landscape and yet, hill farmers are facing their worst economic crisis since the 1930s; average incomes are falling, so that the average hill farmer in 2009 earns £17800 per annum compared to £38600 for the average farmer in England.[19] Bearing in mind that not all farmers are able to diversify into tourist activities, then the plight of so many is parlous indeed and the long term effect on the landscape very worrying.

The 2001 outbreak of Foot and Mouth disease in Cumbria and Northern England may turn out to be a defining moment in the present and future life of farming in the region, particularly hill farming at the margin of profitability. The two most used words in 2001, equally from the lips of farmers, those who live in farming areas, and tourists, were "silent" and "empty." One farmer in Ousby in the Eden Valley described to me the scene from his farm, devoid of all livestock, when he could see six or seven funeral pyres from his farmhouse; he described the scene with a mixture of sadness and bitterness, that the country as a whole, and certainly the Government, failed to understand the plight of hill farmers.

The Foot and Mouth crisis of 2001 brought to the public's notice one indisputable fact that may not have been fully understood by the public and some in government circles. The economy of the Lake District National Park is inextricably linked to the farming and tourism sectors of the economy, for one cannot exist and flourish without the other. If we lose the hill farmers of the National Park and the rest of Cumbria and much of the uplands of northern England, it will not be long before we notice changes in the landscape. Some say that, in less than ten years, the valleys and fells will start to revert to bracken, scrub and trees, and only then will we fully appreciate how valuable was the stewardship role of hill farmers.

In the context of this book, the political arguments can be overlooked, but by no means minimised. The real tragedy of the epidemic in Cumbria and elsewhere was the social misery of farming communities, the impact on tourism and the local community, and the possible long-term damage to the landscape if hill farmers go out of business. Before the Foot and Mouth Crisis, hill farmers were already in a desperate situation. In so many cases there was the danger that this setback might be the final straw. Never before was the general public so aware of the many charities devoted to the welfare of farming communities and the Prince of Wales expressed the fear that some farmers would be driven to consider suicide. Eight years later there is evidence that smaller hill farmers have not returned to sheep farming.

Perhaps the most poignant fact of the crisis was the effect on the traditional Herdwick breed of sheep in Cumbria. This breed of sheep is *hefted* (limited territorially) to the fell on which they are born. Lambs learn their terrain from their mothers and even if bloodlines are saved it will take some time for sheep to become re-hefted to a fell.

Poetry from the crisis

As with every human activity and every emotion common to us all, the 2001 Crisis resulted in some poetry that expressed the emotions felt by farmers and by those who love the valleys and fells of Cumbria. Three examples illustrate this point, the first by James Crowden, the West Country poet and author. He has been a professional soldier, as well as a shepherd and sheep shearer, and writes extensively on farming and rural issues. In a trilogy of poems on Foot and Mouth, titled "Silence at Ramscliffe," he expressed the effect of an outbreak of Foot and Mouth disease on a north Devon farm, affected by the 2001 outbreak. The emotions expressed are, however, common to all farmers, nationwide, who were affected by the outbreak of this terrible disease:

FOOT AND MOUTH
There is fear in the air.
You can feel it climbing over
Hedges
Passing from farm to farm
Invisibly trailing its white coat
Across the fields.

You can hear it crackle
Like a forest fire.
It lives in kitchens
And in the news reports,
In the eyes of children
And in the hunched expressions
Of their animals
Even the dogs have gone wild
With uncertainty. [20]
© *James Crowden*

The second poem is anonymous, appearing on the website of The Catholic Study Circle for Animal Welfare; it is reproduced courtesy of the *Dumfries and Galloway Standard*, first published March 16, 2001[21]:

FOOT AND MOUTH
Why? Oh why have I been born to die?
My ancestors for centuries gone by have
Roamed and grazed these fields and glens
The cries of the curlews, and the tinkling
Of the silver water in the burns was music to
Their ears.
The cries of terror they would hear were
Human: Covenanters, and Levellers.
All I want—it is not much—
Is to suckle my mother, feel her warm tongue
Lick my face, chase my brothers and sisters.
This will never be—
For today my death warrant has been signed

> *By the man from the ministry.*
> *Consolation—if it be—mother, father, brother,*
> *Sister, together on the funeral pyre, will die.*

The final example of someone affected by the 2001 Crisis is from a Veterinary Inspector, who wrote a reflective passage early one morning when he was taking a few hours break from killing animals. The writer is Peter Frost-Pennington[22], a member of the Pennington family, who have owned Muncaster Castle for centuries. He manages the castle as its General Manager. In addition to the following poem, he has written on the lessons to be learned from the 2001 outbreak. The poem is titled "Into the Valleys of Death." It is a poem in free verse and it begins in sombre, reflective mood:

> *Damien Hirst has nothing on me.*
> *I create ghastly pictures of death, officially sanctioned.*
> *I have to believe this mass sacrifice of animals I love is worth it.*
> *Or is it the farmers who are the real sacrifice?*
> *Like the animals, they take it meekly and obediently*
> *Often thanking me for doing it.*
> *After I had killed all 356 cattle in one family's dairy herd*
> *They sent flowers to my wife.*
> *These are the people who are giving up all, in the hope it will save others.*

> *But don't get me wrong*
> *I have now seen plenty of this plague*
> *And it is no common cold.*
> *The animals suffer horribly, as the skin of their tongues peel off*
> *And their feet fall apart.*
> *We must try to kill them quick and clean,*
> *As soon as it appears in a herd or flock.*

> *The farmers' suffering does not end with the visit of the Slaughter men.*

> *I must continue to do my duty*
> *In these Cumbrian killing fields.*
> *Quickly, efficiently and effectively.*

Yes, the official papers must all be in place
Yes, the Health and Safety Man must be happy
Yes, the Environment Agency is only doing their job as best as they can.

It is 6am. Today I go out to kill again.
The worst is the young stock.
I thank God the lambs are not yet born with these ewes today.
I will have to kill a calf born yesterday,
The first beautiful calf from the farmer's pride and joy
His new Charolais bull.

This is not what I trained for.
I hope familiarity will never make me immune from the trauma of killing.
But I do hope—for the animals sake—to be good at it.

It is the virus we are trying to kill!
With our disinfectants and culling policy
Our imprisonment of farmers in their homes
All they have left is the telephone.

Perhaps today there is hope.
One soldier will meet me at the farm gate,
I hope he, not me, will quickly arrange the funeral of the animals I love.
Before their carcases get so bloated they fall apart.
Adding more to the farmers' anguish, trapped amongst them.
I should be free to move on quickly, find the virus
And kill again.

Into the Valley of death drove the 600
Or are now 1100?
The countryside I love is bleeding to death.
Mr Blair, please help.

© Peter Frost-Pennington
23rd March 2001

These observations from someone so closely involved in the epidemic are expressions of extreme sorrow but also of anger.

Cumbria's Farming Landscape

The farming landscape and the farming year of today, would, to some extent, be recognised by Wordsworth and his contemporaries, and when we view the landscape of today, we must realise that we are looking at an historic landscape. There are, inevitably, many changes, particularly in the case of coniferous forest plantations, but the typical hill farm has changed relatively little. Some of the buildings are now derelict or perhaps converted into expensive barn conversions. Some of the mining activity is only seen in disused mines and spoil heaps on the side of valleys, but in essence the hill farm is rooted into the landscape by geography and climate.

The typical hill farm consists of three types of land—Inbye, Intake and Open Fell. Traditionally this arrangement ensures that each farm has a share of valley floor land and open fell.

- **Inbye land** is the most productive and soils are deeper, although often waterlogged and with outcrops of bare rock. Field boundaries are a mixture of dry-stone walls and hedges and usually given over to grazing and grass for hay; fields are generally small and sheep are brought down to inbye lands for mating, lambing and dipping. These fields have often been improved by the use of organic and chemical fertilisers.

- **Intake land** is also enclosed by dry-stone walls and provides rough grazing; fields are larger but contain more bare rock and sometimes areas of woodland, both deciduous and coniferous. Some hill farms have a herd of up to fifty dairy cattle and these are grazed in both the inbye and intake lands. Up to three hundred and fifty sheep, usually the native Herdwick breed, are kept on a typical farm. One limitation on the numbers of livestock is the fact that in severe weather shelter is needed for cows and sheep. The other constraints are the size of the farm and the fertility of the land. In many areas, farming is conducted at the margin of profitability, hence the need for subsidies and other forms of income.

- **Open fell land** is above the intake land and is often common land, and dry-stone walls are only used to border very large areas of fell. Winter weather is too extreme for grazing livestock. Sheep from several farms often graze the open fell and although marking of sheep is used, farmers rely on the fact that Herdwick sheep are hefted to an area of open fell. The loss of such flocks in the foot and mouth epidemic was, therefore, the more tragic, and any compensation awarded to farmers was not a sufficient sum to recompense the long-term loss.

A geographical diversion

Although it is easy to assume that the Lake District farming landscape is the natural landscape of the area, this is far from the case. We all develop a way of viewing landscape, as was discussed earlier in this book, and some of our personal landscapes, we describe as natural, may be the result of centuries of change and development. The Lake District landscape would be very different without the hill farmers and would consist of a mixed deciduous woodland of oak, ash, birch and alder, as well as extensive areas of scrub and bracken. The anxiety over the foot and mouth outbreak and the fear that some farmers would be forced out of business, was partly the result of a concern for the Lakeland environment and landscape that draws thousands of tourists to the area each year.

However, the two critical factors in the Lake District farming system are the landforms and climate of the area. These are the two natural influences on which human management has worked and some mention of these factors is relevant to the theme of this book.

Landforms

The open fells are mostly poor soils and can only support rough grasses and heather, meaning that sheep farming has to be fairly extensive. Many fells have large areas of bare rock outcrops and also waterlogged and boggy vegetation. It is this feature of many fells, that act like a sponge and release water into streams, that explains why the lakes continue to receive water even in the driest months. Notwithstanding this water flow, the level of lakes fluctuates widely between summer and winter.

The valley sides, mostly intake land, are steep especially in those valleys showing the impact of glaciation, as for example in the

Buttermere/Crummock Water valley. The use of machinery on farms is very limited and areas of rock outcrops limit the area of pasture available to farmers. The only areas that are conducive to less extensive farming are the valley floors. Some areas have been drained and improved but the use of machinery is still limited and soils are often thin and infertile and very often very wet and boggy.

Climate

The other limiting factor on Lakeland farming is the Lake District climate, especially in terms of temperature and the length of the growing season. Grass growth is very slow in temperatures of 6^0 Celsius, and this means that, on average, grass in many areas of intake and open fell is not growing between the end of October and mid-April. Sunshine is restricted by cloud cover, and high rainfall causes waterlogging of soils and soil erosion on steep slopes. Cattle normally remain in barns for much of the time between October and April, and sheep are taken off the most exposed open fells.

Climate Statistics for Ambleside: 46 metres above sea level

	J	F	M	A	M	J	J	A	S	O	N	D	Yearly Average
Temperature: °C													
Daily Max	6	7	9	12	16	19	20	19	17	13	9	7	13
Daily Min	0	0	2	4	6	9	11	11	9	6	3	1	5
Average Monthly	3	4	6	8	11	14	15	15	13	10	6	4	9
Rainfall: mm													
Average Monthly Total	214	146	112	101	90	111	134	139	184	196	209	215	1851
Other: average													
Sunshine days per month	20	17	15	15	14	15	18	17	18	19	19	21	208
Hours per day	1.1	2	3.2	4.5	6	5.7	4.5	4.2	3.3	2.2	1.4	1	3.3

These two limiting factors, landforms and climate, mean that farming in the Lake District is nearly always at the margin of profitability.

Hence the need for subsidies and grants from U.K. Government and the European Union, as well as diversification into tourism by many farmers, who open their land to camping and caravans during the summer season, with an increasing number offering bed and breakfast.

This is the point in which to explain that in addition to the factors of landforms and climate, the characteristics of any location are influenced by several other factors:

- Latitude—the Lake District lies between 54^0 North and 55^0 North and on the western seaboard of North West Europe. The moderating influence of the sea and the warming waters of the North Atlantic Drift ensure that summers are cool and winters mild, although there is some evidence that global warming may lead to more stormy weather and colder winters. Ambleside's mean average temperature for January is 3^0 Celsius, whereas Moscow, at a similar latitude, has a mean average temperature of -10^0 Celsius.

- Mid latitude depressions—the prevailing wind for the Lake District is South West to West and the regular passage of low-pressure systems also moderates the temperatures in summer and winter.

- Local temperatures in the Lake District are mainly influenced by altitude, although wind chill can make temperatures, especially on the fells, seem much lower.

- Temperatures in the central lakes can be two or three degrees lower in winter and two or three degrees higher in summer, than locations on the coast.

- Topography can also have an influence on temperature; for example, in winter, frost pockets can develop in valley bottoms creating a temperature inversion.

- Aspect is also important, with south-facing slopes or valley sides having a higher temperature than slopes or valley sides facing north.

The figures above are those for a single location, Ambleside, which is only forty-six metres above sea level and relatively sheltered compared to many areas of the Lake District. All hill farms are at a much higher altitude and local temperatures are mainly influenced by altitude, nearness to the moderating influence of the sea and local topography. Temperatures decrease by about 1.5^0 C with each one hundred fifty metres of ascent and wind speeds also increase with altitude. This is important because the wind chill effect influences farming and the need to bring livestock into shelter in winter.

The Lake District is one of the wettest areas of the United Kingdom. Although Ambleside has an annual average of 1851mm, the village of Seathwaite in Borrowdale has an annual average rainfall of nearly 3300mm, making it the wettest place in England. Comparable figures for Plymouth are 950mm and for London, 593mm. The reasons for the higher totals in the Lake District are first, the western location facing the rain-bearing mid-latitude depressions from the Atlantic Ocean. However, the most significant factor is the relief of the area, giving an orographic effect on the westerly air masses. The eastern side of the Pennines is a rain shadow area with an annual average rainfall of 658mm for Durham.

The novelist Hugh Walpole (1884–1941) lived in Cumberland from 1924 and set his *Herries Chronicle* in the Lake District. The first book in the trilogy, *Rogue Herries* (1930) contains a graphic description of Lake District rain:

> *It was a rain of relentless, determined, soaking, penetrating kind. No other rain anywhere, at least in the British Isles—which have a prerogative of many sorts of rain—falls with so determined a fanatical obstinacy as does this rain. It is not that the sky in any deliberate mood decides to empty itself. It is rain that has but little connection either with earth or with sky, but rather has a life of its own, stern, remorseless and kindly. It falls in sheets of steely straightness, and through it is the rhythm of the beating hammer.*[23]

All who have visited the Lake District often and love its landscape will readily agree with this description. Those who have been turned away from the area by a week or more of heavy rain and overcast skies, may need a little persuading to give the area a second chance! We must, however, remember that the beauty of the Lakes depends on heavy rainfall. The mountain becks look best when in full flow after rain and who does not marvel at the sight of so many waterfalls

194 *Place, Nature and Spirit*

and rushing streams down the side of valleys, glistening in the sunshine after the rain.

In 1807 William Wordsworth opened his "Resolution and Independence," one of the "Poems of the Imagination" with these words after a storm at night:

> *There was a roaring in the wind all night;*
> *The rain came heavily and fell in floods;*
> *But now the sun is rising calm and bright;*
> *The birds are singing in the distant woods;*
> *Over his own sweet voice the Stock-dove broods;*
> *The Jay makes answer as the Magpie chatters;*
> *And all the air is filled with pleasant noise of waters.*
>
> *All things that love the sun are out of doors;*
> *The sky rejoices in the morning's birth;*
> *The grass is bright with rain-drops;—*
> *On the moors*
> *The hare is running races in her mirth;*
> *And with her feet she from the plashy earth*
> *Raises a mist; that glittering in the sun,*
> *Runs with her all the way, wherever she doth run.*

And finally, in part two of the fifteenth of his *Miscellaneous Sonnets* titled "Composed during a Storm," Wordsworth recalls his feelings in Rydal Woods by a torrent:

> *One who was suffering tumult in his soul*
> *Yet failed to seek the sure relief of prayer,*
> *Went forth—his course surrendering to the care,*
> *Of the fierce wind, while mid-day lightnings prowl*
> *Insidiously, untimely thunders growl;*
> *While trees, dim seen, in frenzied numbers, tear*
> *The lingering remnant of their yellow hair,*
> *And shivering wolves, surprised with darkness, howl*
> *As if the sun were not. He raised his eye*
> *Soul-smitten; for that instant, did appear*
> *Large space (mid dreadful clouds) of purist sky,*
> *An azure disk—shield of Tranquillity;*
> *Invisible, unlooked for, minister*

Of providential goodness ever nigh!

This chapter has covered some of the environmental and conservation concerns that face us in the twenty-first century. It is surely apparent that in so many ways the thinking of Wordsworth was concentrated on those things that still concern us today. Many of the issues covered in this chapter would surely have resulted in letters to the editor of the *Daily Telegraph*, the progeny of *The Morning Post* of Wordsworth's day.

Chapter 12
A Special Place and Our Heritage

At the end of the third section of Wordsworth's *Guide to the Lakes,* he wrote of the Lake District as "a sort of national property, in which every man has a right and interest who has an eye to perceive and a heart to enjoy." In this statement there is the clearest indication that the poet saw the area as of national importance. Undoubtedly, he anticipated some of the dangers of mass tourism and its effect on the very beauty of a region that visitors come to enjoy. The tourist term *honey-pot* was unknown to Wordsworth but he was one of the first writers to see future developments that we know all too well in the twenty-first century. His emphasis on the region as of national importance was surely the first stirring of feelings that were to lead to the establishment of the National Trust in 1895 and the National Park in 1951.

The Lake District National Park Authority describes the area as "A Special Place" and sets out the qualities that make it different from Britain's other national parks. Some of these qualities have been at the heart of this book: "the cool, clear lakes, tarns and rivers; ancient woodlands; diverse landscape; the open nature of the fells and its celebrated cultural heritage"[1].

Other national parks have equally important literary associations but none is as closely identified with the birth of Romanticism, when in the space of not much more than fifty years a change took place in the aesthetics of mountain landscapes.

Our appreciation of the Lake District landscape is, in many ways, a legacy of the era of the Romantic poets, painters and writers. The concern for the environment, which is a feature of modern society, is, to some extent, an echo of Romanticism and the desire to appreciate it and conserve it for future generations. There will always be differences of opinion in balancing the needs of the present and the future. In the same way that William Wordsworth saw the coming of the railway to Windermere with a mixture of understanding and disgust, so today there are issues that divide those who argue that development in National Parks is to be avoided in the interest of landscape conservation, and those who argue that there are circumstances where the national interest must take precedence over local environmental concerns.

An example of such an issue that will increase in importance over the next decade or more is the development of wind farms, which, by definition, have to be placed in exposed locations. In a policy document of the National Trust in 2005,[2] we have the dilemma clearly stated. In recognising that the best locations for wind farms are some of the wildest parts of the British Isles, the Trust points out the clash with one of its strategy objectives:

The inspirational qualities of wild areas must not be eroded—the sustainability of society depends on maintaining often elusive components in addition to promoting wholly practical solutions.'

In this strategic plan the National Trust shows that the need for renewable energy generation in the face of an accelerated climate change is clearly recognised. The fact remains that it is difficult to fully reconcile the national need for energy and the preservation of wildness in the National Parks. Our need for wild places has been expressed in many different ways by writers and groups over the last century. The National Trust quotes the words of the American environmentalist, John Muir, (1838–1914),[3] who was born in Scotland:

Thousands of tired, nerve-shaken, over-civilised people are beginning to find…that wilderness is a necessity and that mountain parks and reservations are useful not only as fountains of timber and irrigating rivers, but as fountains of life.

Similarly, the Lake District National Park Authority, in describing the Lake District as "A Special Place,"[4] expresses the same qualities of wild areas and their impact upon the human spirit:

The relatively open character of the uplands, and the lack of modern development, is especially important. To walk freely across the fells, or climb their crags, is liberating and gives a feeling of wildness. To many the Lake District is a place where it is possible to feel remote, yet know the nearest settlement is never far away.

The development of wind farms in such areas needs to balance national needs with the conservation of these landscapes for future generations.

The National Trust document referred to above is titled "A Call for the Wild,"[5] and it sets out the challenges that have to be faced in future years. The arguments put forward by the National Trust do not ignore the fact that more renewable sources of energy are needed, but they do put before the nation the importance of wild areas. A few extracts from the report illustrate the dilemma:

We are facing a global crisis. The consequences of the accelerated climate change which results from the burning of fossil fuels and the clearance of forests worldwide are potentially catastrophic for human, wildlife and environment. In Britain we must be able to influence the global situation, first by implementing ourselves the technologies and the lifestyles which will sustain both environmental and social wellbeing, and then by assisting their take-up elsewhere.

The National Trust is taking an active stance on many environmental matters, including energy conservation and renewable energy generation, and we are worried about the imposition of unsuitable technologies on the wild places of Britain. In the context of all the problems that arise from human activity on the planet, protection of wild places may appear a minor matter. But too often the nation's social and spiritual wellbeing are overlooked in our urgent attempts to sustain wealth and attain environmental security. At a fundamental level, wild places are vital for services like water catchment and recreational space, and they are undoubtedly precious for Britain's threatened biodiversity. However, for many people the greatest value of wild places is as a source of freedom and inspiration.

The above statement is balanced and realistic in its approach and does acknowledge the difficulty of achieving a solution acceptable to all groups. The National Trust also accepts that change is a continuous process, that the landscape we see today is the result of past development and that it is impossible to see the landscape of today as fixed for the future. However, the search for renewable energy resources will have an effect on the wild spaces of the country, particularly the National Parks. The report continues:

> *Since the 1930s UK energy strategy has focussed on the National Grid—this enables coal-fired electricity generation in the Trent valley to feed a Welsh farmhouse; and a Welsh windfarm to feed a Nottinghamshire coalfield settlement. But in Wales, the environment is suffering a double blow—hundreds of wind turbines are intruding on places of value for wildlife and wild landscape; and the pollution from acid rain and nitrogen from coal, oil and gas burning which still forms the bulk of UK energy sources continues unabated.*[6]

One final extract from the 2005 Report is sufficient to illustrate the problems faced by environmental and conservation groups:

> *Under the UN Convention on Climate Change (Kyoto Protocol), the Government has undertaken to deliver 10% of electricity in the UK from non-fossil renewable resources by 2010. This could involve 2000–4000 wind turbines onshore, 1000–3000 turbines offshore and between 100,000 and 300,000 hectares of energy coppice. Even if renewable energy did provide 10% of all electricity delivered, it would still make only a small inroad into total fossil fuel use and greenhouse gas emissions, since the major proportion of fossil fuels are used directly for industry, domestic and commercial space heating, water heating and transport.*[6]

These extracts are from a policy document produced by the National Trust but the views expressed will find common agreement with many other environmental and conservation groups.

"An eye to perceive and a heart to enjoy"

William Wordsworth, who is arguably the greatest of all nature poets, died on the 23rd April 1850, when, no doubt, the daffodils were in bloom throughout the Lake District and especially on the shores of Ullswater. The National Trust was formed in 1895, and three people were largely instrumental in its formation: Canon Hardwicke Drummond Rawnsley, an Anglican clergyman and campaigner for the preservation of the countryside; Miss Octavia Hill, a social reformer; and Sir Robert Hunter, a lawyer.

Canon Rawnsley had earlier been responsible for the formation of the Lake District Defence Society, later to become "The Friends of the Lake District," with Tennyson, Browning, Ruskin and the Duke of Westminster as some of the earliest members. Another campaigner of the time was Beatrix Potter's father, and it was Canon Rawnsley that encouraged the young Beatrix to publish her first book, *The Tale of Peter Rabbit*.

The National Trust, formed in 1895, was not therefore an isolated event but was the result of ideas and campaigning that had begun earlier in the century. Beatrix Potter's father was the first member of the Trust and Canon Rawnsley was Honorary Secretary to the Trust until his death in 1920. Significantly, he was responsible for the campaign that raised the money to buy Brandlehow Wood, 108 acres of pasture and woodland on the western side of Derwentwater, below Catbells. The four oaks planted at the ceremony marking the National Trust's first purchase can still be seen along the road above Brandlehow Wood, as can a commemorative stone.

Canon Rawnsley was born a year after the death of William Wordsworth, and the National Trust was formed forty five years after Wordsworth's death. To what extent can the two men and the ideas that motivated them in their life's work be linked? Certainly Wordsworth saw the Lake District as "a sort of national property," but is it possible to see Wordsworth as a forerunner or inspiration to the movement that was eventually to lead to the formation of the National Trust? There are many grounds to suggest that this would be the case. Wordsworth was a nature poet and was passionate about the preservation of rural values and landscapes. In his poetry, nature was not merely scenery or landscape but a term with spiritual and philosophical importance. However, much of his poetry was rooted in specific locations and, to that extent; he was describing scenery and landscape.

One of the most important writers on Wordsworth and the contribution he made to late nineteenth-century conservation is Stephen Gill,[7] who has written extensively on the subject, particularly in his book, *Wordsworth and the Victorians*. He saw the poet as looking forward to the reasoning and endeavour behind the formation of the National Trust, but also explains that Wordsworthian thinking in forums such as the Wordsworth Society influenced the founders of the National Trust, particularly Canon Rawnsley. The Wordsworth Society was formed in 1880 and numbered 250 individuals at its peak in 1884. In 1882[8] Canon Rawnsley addressed the Wordsworth Society in what Stephen Gill described as "one of the more important documents in the history of conservation in Great Britain because it brought together three ideas" concerned with the preservation and conservation of landscape.

The first concerned the development of the Lake District. In the same way that Wordsworth had protested against the railways coming to Windermere, Canon Rawnsley protested against the railway being extended to Braithwaite and Buttermere. He said, "the vales of Cumberland and Westmorland, charged with the spirit of Wordsworth, must be left…as Nature's own English University in the age of great cities."

John Ruskin, backed by Octavia Hill, joined the protest organised by the Thirlmere Defence Association to prevent the valley being turned into a reservoir to supply water to Manchester. He asked the fundamental question, "Has natural beauty any rights?" Ruskin's comment was more philosophical but the motive was the same:

> *I hold the hills and vales of my native land to be temples of God; and their waves and clouds holier than the dew of the Baptistery, and the incense of the altar.*[9]

Canon Rawnsley's second idea was that all defenders of the Lake District ought to join forces with other organisations. At this stage he saw co-operation between organisations as the goal, but this idea could easily be turned into a call for a national approach to conservation and preservation of landscape. His third idea was even more significant:

> *Some time hence, who knows, a wise Government may enable the Lake District to have a special Act to protect it from railroad outrage for the people, as has been done in the Yosemite Valley of America.*[10]

The comparison with America was good for the campaign for some form of national protection, but in the light of experience, it has never been possible to compare the National Parks of America with our own National Parks. In the Lake District National Park, as with all the others in the United Kingdom, most of the land is owned by many different bodies and individuals; there are towns and villages and an employment structure of great diversity. Our National Parks are wild areas rather than true wilderness reserves.

John Ruskin was an influential character in the development of the National Trust and eventually the National Parks, although Stephen Gill[11] sees Wordsworth as "the originating language and discourse," and it is in the *Guide to the Lakes* that one finds the germ of the National Trust's long gestation. Perhaps one ought to say that the germ was Wordsworth, what he stood for, and what his disciples made of him.

How would William Wordsworth, who has been the inspiration for this book, react if he were able to travel throughout the Lake District in the early years of the twenty-first century? It is, of course, impossible to say, but it is interesting to speculate. He would surely be outraged by the commercialisation of many towns and villages, for example, Windermere and Bowness in August or Hawkeshead, where the car park covers a greater area than the village. He would perhaps have less concern about Grasmere and especially the opening to the public of Dove Cottage and Rydal Mount. He would be impressed and, almost certainly, surprised by the Wordsworth Museum and Art Gallery and the Jerwood Centre that is visited by thousands of Wordsworth pilgrims from around the world.

However, if he were able to visit quiet lakes such as Buttermere or Crummock Water or wander across the open fells, he would, perhaps, be satisfied and proud that part of his legacy has been to preserve such beautiful landscapes. He would, hopefully, see that the area is still "a sort of national property in which every man has a right and interest, who has an eye to perceive and a heart to enjoy."

Epilogue

In Chapter 4 of this book it is suggested that Wordsworth's sonnet, "It is a beauteous evening, calm and free," is a "consideration of the quietness of the human mind as an aspect of the sublime" and leads us in a reverie of silence in the stillness of nature. It is an intensely spiritual and transcendental poem and gives us some understanding of how Wordsworth's spirituality cannot be ignored in much of his greatest poetry.

Wordsworth believed that there is in nature evidence of a Supreme Being and a clear merging of the sublime and the everyday. In that sense it could be said that the spiritual in nature can be seen as evidence of the Divine, even though the viewer may have no orthodox Christian belief. The clearest example of this way of thinking in Wordsworth is seen in his "Tintern Abbey" poem:

> *And I have felt*
> *A presence that disturbs me with the joy*
> *Of elevated thoughts; a sense sublime*
> *Of something far more deeply interfused,*
> *Whose dwelling is the light of setting suns,*
> *And the round ocean and the living air,*
> *And the blue sky, and in the mind of man:*
> *A motion and a spirit, that impels*
> *All thinking things, all objects of all thought,*
> *And rolls through all things.*

In some respects it is, perhaps, an unnecessary, and some may well say, a fruitless task to narrow down Wordsworth's spirituality to either Christian Pantheism or Orthodox Christianity. However, his poetry has a deep spiritual impact upon the reader. This book has concentrated on this aspect of the poet's thinking in some of his greatest poetry.

Two poems are of the utmost importance in coming to an appreciation of the development of Wordsworth's spiritual thinking. The first is the 1804 poem referring to the period of childhood:

My heart leaps up when I behold
A rainbow in the sky:
So was it when my life began;
So is it now I am a man;
So be it when I shall grow old,
Or let me die!
The child is the father of the Man;
And I could wish my days to be
Bound each to each by natural piety.

Wordsworth was thirty-four years old when he composed this poem. He remembered the way he thought as a child and in looking back he realised that these few lines were still relevant, especially to him, as an adult. It reminds us that our thinking as adults is, to a greater or lesser extent, determined by childhood experiences. We may become wiser as a result of learning and by our life experiences, but our childhood thinking may remain with us throughout our life. The cynic may say that any form of nostalgia is simply looking back on a golden age that almost certainly never existed. However, is it not possible that our thinking as adults is determined by earlier experiences as a child? It is clear that Wordsworth thought along these lines.

The last three lines of this poem are used as a preface to Wordsworth's greatest spiritual poem, "Ode, Intimations of Immortality from Recollections of Early Childhood."

If we accept the premise that we look back on our childhood as a golden age, then it is natural that we ask what has been lost as we grow into adults. The last line of the first stanza of the ode is surely referring to the quality of our seeing; it may be nostalgia but, equally, it may be something deeper:

There was a time when meadow, grove, and stream,
The earth, and every common sight,
To me did seem
Apparelled in celestial light,
The glory and the freshness of a dream.

It is not now as it hath been of yore;—
Turn wheresoe'er I may,
By night or day,
The things which I have seen I now can see no more.
(Stanza 1)

Wordsworth still saw all these things as an adult, but he felt that some of their glory had been diminished in adult life. Is it not possible that this was the reason why, in so much of his poetry, he saw an idealized landscape, some critics may say, a sanitised landscape. The second stanza of the ode records the poet's belief "that there hath past away a glory from the earth." The mature Wordsworth was still moved and inspired by animate and inanimate nature, but he desired a return to the thoughts he had experienced as a child. Nature was still supreme but at the end of stanza 3, Wordsworth called to his mind, the memories of childhood:

Thou Child of Joy,
Shout round me, let me hear thy shouts, thou happy
Shepherd-boy.

The poet remained a child of nature and acknowledged that he had experienced nature in all its glory, "the fullness of your bliss." However, even in the knowledge of all that nature displays, there is a looking back to something that has been lost. As children we have an instinctive wisdom that is easily lost as adults.

The fifth stanza is particularly important and shows us some of the complex spiritual beliefs that go some way to understanding Wordsworth's deepest thoughts:

Our birth is but a sleep and a forgetting:
The Soul that rises with us, our life's Star,
Hath had elsewhere its setting,
And cometh from afar:
Not in entire forgetfulness,
And not in utter nakedness,
But trailing clouds of glory do we come
From God, who is our home:
Heaven lies about us in our infancy!
Shades of the prison-house begin to close
Upon the growing Boy,

> *But He beholds the light, and whence it flows,*
> *He sees it in his joy;*
> *The youth, who daily farther from the east*
> *Must travel, still is Nature's Priest,*
> *And by the vision splendid*
> *Is on his way attended;*
> *At length the Man perceives it die away,*
> *And fade into the light of common day.*
> *(Stanza 5)*

This stanza displays much of the spiritual thinking of Wordsworth as a mature poet. There are strong references to the Platonic belief in pre-existence. Plato believed that the Soul had an existence before birth and on the death of the individual the Soul returned to an ideal state. Is Wordsworth suggesting that as children we retain some memory of Paradise, and therefore the child is the obvious choice as "Nature's Priest"? Wordsworth's spirituality is a mixture of traditional Christian belief in an immortal soul and an un-biblical belief that we come from some kind of presence with God. In addition, he believed that we experience something of heaven in our childhood that is lost as we become adults: "Shades of the prison house begin to close upon the growing boy." There is a sense of melancholy in our adult life and a yearning for something we felt as children that is lost as we become adults. Wordsworth is saying that we have an awareness of the immortality of the Soul that is felt when we are children, less so when we are adults:

> *The Child is Father of the Man:*
> *And I could wish my days to be*
> *Bound each to each by natural piety.*

These themes run all through the "Immortality" ode and can be seen in many different places. The adult mind knows that our life is a search for meaning, and yet, underlying all, there is the awareness that life is finite and that during our life we are trying to get back to our thinking and experiences as children. As we grow from childhood to maturity we become aware of our mortality and the course of our life:

> *A wedding or a festival,*
> *A mourning or a funeral;*
> *(Stanza 7)*

At the heart of stanza 8, the poet reveals that our life's search for meaning is tempered by the realisation that life is finite and that during our life we are trying to get back to our thinking and experiences as children:

> *Mighty Prophet! Seer blest!*
> *On whom those truths do rest,*
> *Which we are toiling all our lives to find,*
> *In darkness lost, the darkness of the grave.*

Wordsworth continued in the "Ode" to meditate on the mind of a child and that of an adult. He described our childhood experiences as a source of "perpetual benediction." The sense of loss is still there but it is not always the loss of everyday things and experiences, but rather for "those obstinate questionings of sense and outward things…those first affections, those shadowy recollections."

The essential nature of Wordsworth's looking back to childhood is that we try to retain memories of childhood even as we realise our mortality. We all look back on our childhood with a certain wistfulness, even melancholy, but as adults, we have to accept that the joy and expectation of childhood has gone, perhaps, beyond recall:

> *What though the radiance which was once so bright*
> *Be now for ever taken from my sight,*
> *Though nothing can bring back the hour*
> *Of splendour in the grass, of glory in the flower;*
> *We will grieve not, rather find*
> *Strength in what remains behind;*
> *In the primal sympathy*
> *Which having been must ever be;*
> *(Part of stanza 10)*

Even as we remember our childhood, we also, as adults, realise our mortality. At the end of stanza 10, we find the first expression of immortality: "In the faith that looks through death."

In conclusion, the "Immortality" ode is saying to us that the joy, peace and inspiration of nature remains. Gone are the experiences and emotions of youth, but the beauty of nature remains, for nature is eternal. The final stanza is the most joyous, and, although the melancholy is part of our life as adults, the poet has come to a

210 *Place, Nature and Spirit*

resolution of his questioning concerning the meaning of life and with that resolution comes a feeling of peace and tranquillity:

And O, ye Fountains, Meadows, Hills, and Groves,
Forebode not any severing of our loves!
Yet in my heart of hearts I feel your might;
I only have relinquished one delight
To live beneath your more habitual sway.
I love the Brooks which down their channels fret,
Even more than when I tripped lightly as they;
The innocent brightness of a new-born Day
Is lovely yet;

The clouds that gather round the setting sun
Do take a sober colouring from an eye
That hath kept watch o'er man's mortality;
Another race hath been, and other palms are won.
Thanks to the human heart by which we live,
Thanks to its tenderness, its joys, and fears,
To me the meanest flower that blows can give
Thoughts that do often lie too deep for tears.

The link to passages in his "Tintern Abbey" poem is unmistakeable, especially in the last stanza of the "Immortality" ode. The "thoughts that do often lie too deep for tears" are a clear link to the thoughts of Wordsworth in his 1798 "Tintern Abbey" poem:

For I have learned
To look on nature, not as in the hour
Of thoughtless youth; but hearing oftentimes
The still sad music of humanity,
Nor harsh nor grating, though of ample power
To chasten and subdue. And I have felt
A presence that disturbs me with the joy
Of elevated thoughts; a sense sublime
Of something far more deeply interfused,
Whose dwelling is the light of setting suns,
And the round ocean and the living air,
And the blue sky, and in the heart of man.

This book makes no claim to be a work of scholarship, although it makes use of some of the most scholarly works on Wordsworth and his poetry. It is an, unashamedly, personal statement, not just on William Wordsworth and his life and poetry but also on the changing aesthetics of landscape that was part of the Romantic era. The book has considered the thinking of the time with an emphasis on the spiritual aspects of the period and, especially, in the poetry of Wordsworth. It is wrong to see Wordsworth simply as a poet of place, although few doubt that Wordsworth was the finest poet of the Lake District. There are far deeper aspects of his poetry that still challenge us today and that reach the deepest recesses of the soul.

If the reader is encouraged by this book to look more closely at Wordsworth's poetry and that an individual's appreciation of the Lake District is enhanced, then the author will have achieved far more than he expected at the start of the book. The final words must be from the conclusion of Wordsworth's *Guide to the Lakes*:

> *The Lake District is a sort of national property, in which every man has a right and interest who has an eye to perceive and a heart to enjoy.*

References

Chapter 1   Beginnings

1. Bailey, Patrick (1980) Geographical Association
2. BBC (2005) Television series – *A Picture of Britain* – presented by David Dimbleby.
3. Reviewer of the first programme – *A Picture of Britain* "The Romantic North", Serena Davies – Arts 'Telegraph' 28th May 2005.
4. David W. Jardine (1997) "To Dwell with a Boundless Heart: On the Integrated Curriculum and the Recovery of the Earth" Chapter 20 in *The Curriculum Studies Reader*, edited by David J. Flinders and Stephen L. Thornton.
5. ibid 4

Chapter 2   Personal Landscapes

1. Hope Nicolson, Marjorie (1959) *Mountain Gloom and Mountain Glory. The Development of the Aesthetics of the Infinite.* Cornell University. W.W. Norton & Company Inc. New York. (1963)
2. Gold, John R. and Burgess, Jacqueline. (1982) Eds. *Valued Environments*. Chapter 4, Shoard, Marion "The Lure of the Moors."
3. Chiang, Yee, (1937) *The Silent Traveller – A Chinese Artist in Lakeland* – page 30 on Derwentwater.
4. Psalm 104 v 24. Authorised Version 1611.
5. Nicholson, Norman (1948) "The Seven Rocks."
6. Lovelock, James (1979) *Gaia: A new look at life on earth.*

Chapter 3   William Wordsworth and his times

1. The "Terror" was the period of the French Revolution between mid-1793 and July 1794 when Robespierre organised the execution of anyone opposed to the regime.
2. Canon H.D.Rawnsley (1883) "Address to the Wordsworth Society: The Proposed Permanent Lake District Defence Society."
3. Wordsworth's second letter to the Editor of the *Morning Post*.
4. Martineau, Harriet (1855) *Complete Guide to the Lakes*.
5. Martineau, Harriet (1855) *Complete Guide to the Lakes*. Quoted in Nicholson, Norman (1955) 'The Lakers'.
6. Canon H.D. Rawnsley (1883) "Address to the Wordsworth Society."
7. Professor John Stuart Blackie, Professor of Greek, University of Edinburgh 1809–1895
8. Sir Frederic Leighton, President of the Royal Academy 1878–1896
9. ibid 6

Chapter 4   Fearful Landscapes

1. Walpole, Horace (1793) *Letters*, ed. by Mrs Paget Toynbee (Oxford 1903) the letter is dated from Aix in Savoy, September 30, 1793)
2. *Beowulf* in Modern English, trans. by Mary E. Waterhouse (Cambridge 1949) pp. 48–49.
3. Tolkien, J.R.R. (1954) Chapter 3 of Book 1, *The Fellowship of the Ring*. Volume 1 of the trilogy, *The Lord of the Rings*. George Allen & Unwin.
4. Nicolson, Marjorie Hope (1959) *Mountain Gloom and Mountain Glory. The Development of the Aesthetics of the Infinite*. Cornell University.
5. Shama, Simon (1996) *Landscape and Memory*. Fontana Press.

6. Burnet, Thomas (1684) *The Sacred Theory of the Earth*, trans. from Latin.
7. Rosa, *Salvator to Ricciardi*, May 13, 1662 (Rome 1939)
8. Rosa, *Salvator*, ibid.
9. William Gell (1797) *A Tour of the Lakes 1797*, published in 2000 by Smith Settle Ltd. edited by William Rollinson.
10. Wordsworth, William, "Descriptive Sketches" 1792.
11. Wordsworth, William – see Russell Noyes (1973) *Wordsworth and the Art of Landcape*
12. Ibid. Note 2 of chapter 2. See "Valued Environments" chapter 4 by Marion Shoard.
13. Woodring, Carl (1989) *Nature and Art – cultural transformations in Nineteenth Century Britain.*
14. Ibid 13.
15. Ibid 6.
16. Wordsworth, William (1845) *Miscellaneous Sonnets*, number 30.

Footnote: Thoughts on: *Mountain Gloom and Mountain Glory.*

1. Marjorie, Hope Nicolson, Chapter 1: "The Literary Heritage."
2. Giles Fletcher, (1549–1611)
3. Charles Cotton, *Poems*, ed. by John Beresford (New York, n.d.) pp. 45–47.
4. William Wordsworth "Lines Written a Few Miles above Tintern Abbey, on Revisiting the Banks of the Wye during a Tour, July 13, 1798."
5. Andrew Marvell "Upon Appleton House" *Poems and Letters*, ed. by H.M. Margoliouth, (Oxford 1927) 1, 72 and 82.
6. John Donne, "The First Anniversary" ii 284.
7. Louis Ginzberg, *The Legends of the Jews* (Philadelphia 1913) p 142.
8. Ibid 7

9. Thomas Burnet *The Sacred Theory of the Earth*, 1, 394.
10. John Calvin, *The Institute of the Christian Religion* 1, pp. 58, 61 and 69 (New Haven, 1816)
11. James Thomson "Seasons," *Complete poetical Works*, ed. by J.L. Robertson (Oxford 1908)
12. Marjorie Hope Nicolson, page 329, Norton Library edition 1963.
13. James Thomson, "Winter" ii pp. 845–846.
14. James Thomson, "Liberty" iv, pp. 344–349.
15. William Wordsworth, *Guide to the Lakes* London 1835 page 99.
16. Marjorie Hope Nicolson, *Epilogue* page 381.

Chapter 5   In search of the spiritual

1. Gill, Stephen Gill (1998) *Wordsworth and the Victorians*
2. Wyatt, John (1995) *Wordsworth and the Geologists*
3. Dean, Dennis (1968) Ph.D.dissertation on "Geology and English literature: Crosscurrents 1770–1830." The University of Wisconsin
4. ibid, chapter 3
5. ibid, chapter 3
6. John Ray I (London 1691)
7. Douglas J. Porteous (1996) Environmental Aesthetics – ideas, politics and planning"
8. Ryan, Robert M. (2005) "Wordsworthian Science in the 1870s." *Wordsworth Circle* 36(2) Spring 2005
9. Thompson, Ian H. (2007) *William Wordsworth, Landscape Architect*. Wordsworth Circle, September 22nd 2007
10. Ibid 7
11. *The Economist* 21st December 1996, Leader article, "Godliness and Greenness"

Nigel Hammett 217

12. William Wordsworth, *Poems referring to the period of children,* Number 1 (1804)
13. *Faiths for the Future*, ed. Robert Vint, Religious and Moral Education Press (1988)
14. Passmore, John, *Man's Responsibility for Nature*, New York: Scriber 1974
15. Francis of Assisi, founder of the Franciscan Order. "Canticle of Brother Sun" (13th Century)
16. ibid 10 of Chapter 4 'Footnote'
17. Sir Matthew Hale (1609–1676). *Journal of Historical Geography*, Vol. 21–23 "The Ethics of Environmental Concern" Robin Attfield (1983)
18. Reith Lectures 2000 "Respect for the Earth" Lecture 6 by the Prince of Wales, *A Royal View* BBC 2000
19. ibid
20. Rachel Carson *Silent Spring* (Boston, Houghton Mifflin 2002) 40th Anniversary Edition
21. ibid

Chapter 6   Wordsworth and the Bliss of Solitude

1. Jonathan Bate *Romantic Ecology. Wordsworth and the Environmental Tradition* (1991) Chapter 4: 'The Naming of Places'.
2. William Wordsworth – "Lines Written a few Miles above Tintern abbey, on Revisiting the Banks of the Wye during a Tour," July 13, 1798.
3. Ibid
4. Laurence Goldstein (1977) *Ruins and Empire: The Evolution of a Theme in Augustan and Romantic Literature* page 183.
5. Dorothy Wordsworth *The Grasmere Journal* Thursday 15th April. Michael Joseph illustrated edition 1987.
6. Ibid.
7. Quoted in *Wordsworth A Life* 2000 Juliet Barker. Viking. Quoted from *The Fenwick Notes of William*

Wordsworth ed. by Jared Curtis (Bristol Classical Press 1993)
8. Christopher Wordsworth, *Memoirs of William Wordsworth* (2 vols, London 1851)
9. William Gilpin *Observations on the River Wye* 1782.
10. Jonathan Bate (1992) "Romantic Ecology Revisited – New York Conference 'Green Romanticism.'" Reviewed in *Wordsworth Circle* 24(3) Summer 1993
11. Harriet Martineau (1855) *Complete Guide to the Lakes.*
12. ibid
13. Carter, R. and Bailey, P. (1996) "Geography in the Whole Curriculum" in Bailey, P. and Fox, P. (eds.) *Geography Teacher Handbook' Sheffield: Geographical Association*, pp. 11–27
14. John Donne (1572–1691) "Devotions upon Emergent Occasions, Meditation 17"

Chapter 7   The Lake District and the Spirit of Place

1. Lowenthal, D and Prince, H.C. (1964) "The English Landscape." *Geographical Review* 54 pp. 309–346.
2. Lowenthal, D. and Prince, H.C. (1964) "English Landscape tastes." *Geographical Review* 55 pp. 186–222
3. J.K. Knight (1966) Geopiety refers to the emotional bond or awareness (piety) that people have towards space (geo). "Notes on early American Geopiety" in *Human Nature in geography.* (Cambridge 1966)
4. Yi-Fu-Tuan (1974) *Topophilia: a study of Environmental Perception, Attitudes and Values.* Prentice Hall.
5. *Prose Works of William Wordsworth* ed. Alexander B. Grosart (1876)
6. Foakes, R.A. "Beyond the Visible World: Wordsworth and Coleridge" in *Lyrical Ballads* in *Romanticism: the Journal of Romantic Culture and Criticism.* 5.1 (1999)

7. Dean, Dennis (1968) Ph.D. dissertation – The University of Wisconsin "Geology and English Literature: Crosscurrents 1770–1830."
8. John Wyatt (1995) *Wordsworth and the Geologists*. Cambridge.
9. Witherick, Michael, Ross, Simon and Small, John (2001) *A Modern Dictionary of Geography*. (Arnold)
10. Wordsworth, William (1835) *Guide to the Lakes* Excursions, page 167 of the 1984 edition, Webb & Bower.
11. Radcliffe, Ann (1794) *The Mysteries of Udolpho*.
12. Mc Cracken, David (1984) *Wordsworth and the Lake District*. (OUP 1984)
13. Radcliffe, Ann (1795) "The Jaws of Borrowdale" from *A Journey Made in the Summer of 1794*. See page 565 in Wu, Duncan (1994) 'Romanticism: An Anthology'.
14. Mac Lean, Kenneth (1970) *Agrarian Age – a background for Wordsworth*, page 24
15. Brownlow, Timothy (1983) *John Clare and Picturesque Landscape*
16. William Gilpin (1792) *Observations on the western part of England.*
17. William Knight and Uvedale Price – quoted in Russell Noyes (1973) *Wordsworth and the Art of Landscape*
18. Russell Noyes (1973) *Wordsworth and the Art of Landscape*
19. Ibid 6

Chapter 8   Lordly and Majestic Duddon

1. *History and Directory of Furness and Cumberland* P. Mannex & Co (1882)
2. Thompson, B.L (1946) *The Lake District and the National Trust*.
3. Hughes, Felicity (2004) *William Wordsworth and the Wonderful Walker*.

4. Dean, Dennis (1968) Ph.D. dissertation – The University of Wisconsin – "Geology and English Literature: Crosscurrents 1770–1830."
5. *Prose Works of William Wordsworth for the first time collected* e book ISO – 8859 – 1. Also Ed. W.J.B. Owen and Worthington Smyser, Jane (1974) *The Prose Works of William Wordsworth.*
6. Cooper, J.C. (date c 1970) *Duddon Valley History* – Section 2 "Crafts of the Duddon Valley."
7. Noyes, Russell (1973) *Wordsworth and the Art of Landscape.*

Chapter 9   Another Cumbrian Poet

1. Nicholson, Norman, in *The River's Voice: An Anthology of Poetry* by Common Ground.
2. Ray, John (London 1691) "The wisdom of God Manifested in the Work of Creation."
3. Gardner, Phillip (1973) Norman Nicholson (Twayne's English Authors series, TEAS 153. Quoting the 1952 broadcast by Norman Nicholson.

Chapter 10   National Parks: The Wilderness Experience

1. Michael Witherick, Simon Ross and John Small (2001) *A Modern Dictionary of Geography.* Arnold.
2. Stephen Daniels (1993) *Fields of Vision.* Princeton University Press.
3. Tom Stephenson (1978) quoted in John R. Gold and Jacqueline Burgess (1982) *Valued Environments.*
4. John R. Gold and Jacqueline Burgess (1982) *Valued Environments*, Chapter 1, "On the Significance of Valued Environments." Harper Collins publishers Ltd.
5. National Trust (2001) *Wessex News* Summer 2001
6. Marion Shoard (1982) in "Valued Environments" – ibid 4
7. Gerald McGuire ibid 4

8. C.E.M. Joad (1937 essay) ibid 4
9. Anne Bronte (1836) Verses by Lady Geralda
10. *Geographical Magazine* 1971 survey

Chapter 11   Past, Present and Future

1. Sonnet: "On the projected Kendal and Windermere Railway" William Wordsworth. 1844.
2. William Wordsworth *Guide to the Lakes* 1835 edition, third section – "Changes, and Rules of Taste for Preventing their Bad Effects."
3. Ibid
4. Ibid
5. Ibid (first recorded in the 1810 edition)
6. Merlin Winterson *The National Trust: The First Hundred Years* (1994) page 44. BBC Books and National Trust
7. North York Moors National Park, Education Service (1998) – in notes on "The National Parks of England and Wales"
8. Forestry Commission (1998) "A New Focus for England's Woodlands"
9. Forestry Commission (1998) ibid
10. William Gell (1797) 'A Tour of the Lakes'.
11. *The Prose Works of William Wordsworth*, ed. Rev. Alexander Grosart. Echo library 2006 – Wordsworth's "Descriptions of the scenery of the Lakes"
12. William Wordsworth "Poems founded on the Affections" (1800) – "The Brothers"
13. United Utilities, The National Trust and the Forestry Commission (2000) – "Wild Ennerdale Partnership"
14. National Trust and the Wild Ennerdale Partnership
15. *National Trust Magazine* Summer 2004
16. William Wordsworth *Guide to the Lakes* 1835 edition. Page 67 of the *Guide* (1984). Webb & Bower.

17. Ibid 11. Page 273 of *The Prose Works of William Wordsworth* Ed. Rev. Alexander Grosart.
18. Ibid 2 page 284
19. *Westmorland Gazette* 2nd November 2009
20. James Crowden – "Foot and Mouth" (2001)
21. Anonymous poem on the website of The Catholic Study Circle for Animal Welfare– reproduced by courtesy of the *Dumfries and Galloway Standard*
22. Peter Frost Pennington (2001) "Foot and Mouth – into the Valley of Death"
23. Hugh Walpole (1930) *Rogue Herries* – the first book in the Herries Chronicle series.

Chapter 12   A Special Place and Our Heritage

1. Lake District National Park Authority (2005) "A Special place"
2. National Trust policy on wind farms—August 2005 "A Call for the Wild"
3. John Muir (1938–1914) quoted in "A Call for the Wild" ibid 2
4. LDNPA "A Special Place" ibid 1
5. National Trust (2005) "A Call for the Wild" ibid 2
6. ibid 2
7. Stephen Gill (1998) *Wordsworth and the Victorians*.
8. Wordsworth Society (1882) Canon Rawnsley—address to the Wordsworth Trust; a copy exists in the Trust's Library at Grasmere
9. John Ruskin (1878) "Has natural beauty any rights?" Records of the Thirlmere Defence Association.
10. Canon Rawnsley (1882) ibid 8
11. Ibid 7